The Soul of Civil Society

The Soul of Civil Society

*Voluntary Associations and the
Public Value of Moral Habits*

Don Eberly and Ryan Streeter

LEXINGTON BOOKS
Lanham • Boulder • New York • Oxford

LEXINGTON BOOKS

Published in the United States of America
by Lexington Books
A Member of the Rowman & Littlefield Publishing Group
4720 Boston Way, Lanham, Maryland 20706

PO Box 317
Oxford
OX2 9RU, UK

British Library Cataloguing in Publication Information Available

Library of Congress Cataloging-in-Publication Data

Eberly, Don E.
    The soul of civil society : voluntary associations and the public value of moral habits / Don
Eberly, Ryan Streeter.
        p. cm.
    Includes bibliographical references and index.
    ISBN 0-7391-0423-3 (cloth : alk. paper) — ISBN 0-7391-0424-1 (paper : alk. paper)
    1. Voluntarism—United States. 2. Associations, institutions, etc.—United States. 3. Non-
governmental organizations—United States. 4. Social problems—United States. 5. Social
ethics—United States. 6. United States—Moral conditions. 7. United States—Social conditions.
I. Streeter, Ryan, 1969– II. Title.

    HN90.V64 E24 2002
    361.3'7—dc21   2002008110

Printed in the United States of America

♾™ The paper used in this publication meets the minimum requirements of American National
Standard for Information Sciences—Permanence of Paper for Printed Library Materials,
ANSI/NISO Z39.48–1992.

Contents

Introduction

Voluntary Associations and the Primacy of Moral Habits

Ryan Streeter

Habits That Serve the Public

Upon hearing that his father, the emperor, has decided to anoint another as successor to the throne, the son looks at his father and weeps, "You wrote to me once, 'Esteem the four chief virtues: wisdom, justice, fortitude, and temperance.' As I read the list, I knew I had none of them." The emperor ruefully confesses that his son's failures in virtue are owing to his failures as a father, and yet his decision remains: he will appoint a valiant general to take his throne. The reason? Because, in the emperor's words, his son "is not a moral man. He cannot rule; he *must not* rule." The general, on the other hand, should become emperor because he has mastered the public virtues and remained free from corruption.

This scene is from the 2000 DreamWorks blockbuster, *Gladiator*. The son, Commodus, eventually murders his father, Marcus Aurelius, and appoints himself emperor of Rome. The general, Maximus, loses his family to Commodus's ruthless sword and ends up a slave and a gladiator. The film becomes a tale of virtue. Maximus, a man marked by piety and familial devotion, embodies each of the four cardinal virtues at various points in his quest to bring the impious, vicious Commodus to justice. Maximus, in the end, restores dignity to the republic of Rome not through money or political power or gladiatorial success alone, but through the Roman ideal of the steady, habitual application of virtues.

Gladiator's appeal is not merely in its dramatic gladiator contests or grand sets but in its portrayal of the rewards of virtue and the failures of vice. It appeals to our sentiments that tell us it is better to contribute to the good of the community than to satisfy our petty desires. It appeals to our deep sense that a nation's success rests not in its money or power but in its goodness. And it appeals to our understanding that moral stability has public, and not merely private, value.

Americans care about the public value of moral habits. Perhaps uniquely, we have a tendency to look to the moral causes of social dysfunctions. We want to know which behaviors, habits, and practices carry a social cost. As Gertrude Himmelfarb has pointed out, if Americans look at social problems such as single parenthood or welfare dependency with less permissiveness than other countries, "it is because we pride ourselves on being not only the most democratic nation but also the most moral one ('Moralistic,' our denigrators would say)."[1] For all our moral confidence, however, we are somewhat timid in our understanding, or acknowledgment, of the environments, institutions, and forms of association that cultivate the kinds of habits that make society healthy.

This book is about the role that voluntary associations and the basic institutions of a civil society play in cultivating moral, or civic, habits. Moral habits are more than moral beliefs, "views," or "frameworks"—which can be defended by argument or imposed on others. Moral habits are lived more than defended (or perhaps their defense is in their practice), and they contribute to the well-being of others. They consist of repeated behaviors such as sacrifice, restraint, generosity, good judgment, fairness, and productiveness.

They can be collectively referred to as "civility," which, in the words of the late University of Chicago professor Edward Shils, "is an attitude and a pattern of conduct" rooted in "respect for the dignity and the desire for dignity of other persons."[2] Yale University's Stephen Carter, likewise, defines "civility" as "the sum of the many sacrifices we are called to make for the sake of living together."[3] Civility is, in essence, a collection of the habits on which our democratic way of life depends. As Carter points out, civility is not merely about politeness, as many of us might think, but is so intertwined with morality itself that a "crisis of civility . . . is part of a larger crisis of morality."[4] Thus to care about civic habits is one and the same thing as caring about moral habits.

The primary public value of voluntary associations, as this book argues, is that they create environments in which civility—and thus moral habits—can be fostered. They are, in Edmund Burke's words, the "little platoons" in which the seeds of a healthy democracy are planted. He wrote that to "be attached to the subdivision, to love the little platoon we belong to in society, is the first principle (the germ as it were) of public affections. It is the first link in the series by which we proceed toward a love to our country and to mankind."[5]

Burke and many of his eighteenth-century peers understood that small-scale, local associations impart the most important first step in loyalty to others, engagement in one's community, and eventually love of country: they shape our affections and make us inclined to see value in sacrificing for others and our communities. Once this happens, the habits of democracy follow. We begin to treat our responsibility to others not merely as a duty to be grudgingly performed, but as a heartfelt expectation of ourselves and neighbors. Patriotism begins at home, in the neighborhood, at church, in the voluntary association.

The Primacy of Moral Habits

The past fifteen years have seen an explosion of literature on the importance of the voluntary (or "independent" or "third" or "nonprofit") sector of society, which is commonly defined as the realm of civil society. With all the attention civil society has received in recent years, it may be asked, why another book on the topic? Are people not already persuaded that the voluntary sector is important?

The uniqueness of the present book is in its focus on moral health. It argues that the moral condition of America, for which the majority of American citizens repeatedly express concern, can be greatly strengthened through our involvement in voluntary associations. Moral habits are not learned in the same way that ethics are learned in an ethics course or book; rather, we learn them by being put in situations where we have to practice them. The voluntary sector, where we freely join up with other people in what Jean Bethke Elshtain calls the "sturdy but resilient institutions of democratic civil society," often prompts us toward acts of generosity, mutual assistance, self-sacrifice, and compassion—which we would not otherwise undertake in the workplace or during the course of an average day.[6] American greatness hangs not only upon a successful market and a strong government but upon the cultivation of humane and moral habits in the voluntary sector.

The recent revival of interest in civil society has followed two main tracks. Many commentators, on the one hand, have rightly been concerned about the memberlessness of American society. Individualism, it has been widely noted, hinders civic engagement and produces a general civic anomie. These commentators, whose perspective we might call "communitarian," argue that civic engagement will cure us of individualism's harmful effects. Often, however, this argument turns into advocacy for a greater "sense of community" only. Community, we sometimes forget, is more than the passive act of belonging to a group or enjoying high levels of social capital; it is the product of giving, hard work, self-sacrifice, and give-and-take.

The trouble with the overly communitarian interest in the voluntary sector is that it is often thin. For one thing, a "sense of community" is an effect of something else, something more primary and important—namely the obligation we feel for others that prompts us to act virtuously and on their behalf. Communitarian writings sometimes look to renew older forms of association but without older forms of morality, mainly because "old" morality is usually conceived only in terms of coercive and paternalistic forms of social authority. Communitarians generally argue for newer, more relaxed and pluralistic moralities.

What this view too often misses, however, is that no "new" morality is really needed. What we more likely need—and what is more likely practicable—is an ongoing effort to feed and strengthen the moral habits on which we have long depended. Generosity, fairness, restraint, and productiveness, for instance, are nothing new; nor are they intrinsically linked to coercive and authoritarian moralities; nor do many people need to be persuaded that they are good.

In the second train of thought, civil society revivalists have rightfully argued that community-oriented voluntary associations will help make services to low-income families more effective. Truly, churches, neighborhood groups, and community-building nonprofits have immense value in our continuing fight against poverty. They are closer to families in need than conventional social services providers, and they are likely to be able to make moral claims on individuals when necessary.

In all our enthusiasm to promote and defend this view, however, we often neglect discussions about the other side of the equation, namely that the moral value of community-based involvement is just as important in the case of volunteers, board members, funders, and others involved in managing and administering the work of civil society. Community-based organizations, in their copious varieties and purposes, are incubators of publicly valid moral habits for more than the recipients of their services. They are first and foremost, again to cite Elshtain, about creating citizens rather than solving problems, so much so that "without [them] there is no democratic culture."[7] Civil society is morally important for all Americans and not merely those living in poverty.

In short, for all the progress we have made in heightening the public importance of civil society, we cannot forget that there is more to the voluntary sector than creating richer community or more effective services. Its essence is in its unique capacity for fostering the habits of citizenship, which are, to be true, moral to the core. The cultivation of restraint, responsibility, and the other humane habits on which democracy and a healthy public spirit depend is a chief, yet underarticulated, contribution the voluntary sector makes to our society.

Civil society cannot be morally neutral. Its institutions can go wrong. Recent events have painfully shown us that rogue nongovernmental organizations can be used to support networks of terror bent on destroying democratic society. We must appreciate civil society's moral value for what it is and vigilantly protect its capacity for cultivating democratic citizens. It is a fundamental safeguard against the enemies of goodness, fairness, opportunity, and progress. The recent outpouring of civic strength and goodness in the United States following murderous acts of terror is a testament to the moral strength of American citizenship.

The growing respect that many Americans have for the role of civil society in our culture thus needs to be buttressed by a clear awareness of the contribution moral habits make to public life. Through our primary associations, from families to grassroots nonprofits to congregations to active professional associations, we cultivate a moral climate that most Americans consider desirable. The voluntary sector, more than any other sector in society, possesses the capability to train our moral sensibilities and develop in us an active respect for the dignity of others.

Key Themes

In making its point that America's general health depends in large measure upon the under-appreciated moral habits of its people, this book relies upon several underlying themes.

Moral habits contribute to the public good. Moral habits, or what we sometimes refer to as virtues, are behaviors that strengthen the community, make our neighborhoods better, and contribute to society's well-being. Too often, we associate the word "moral" either with personal piety, the public expression of which is negligible, or with a kind of self-righteousness, the public expression of which is usually judgmental and divisive.

This book unabashedly argues that some habits, such as benevolence and restraint, are better than others in terms of what they contribute to the good of the community. This book also argues that our society is in need of a renewed interest in manners and the Golden Rule. Moral habits are not simply a private matter. They are "caught" in human association more than "taught" by any particular morality. As such, they have public significance and should be a regular part of public discussion, which has for too long tried to hide behind the thin veil of value neutrality.

The individual-community dichotomy is superficial. This book argues against the effects of excessive individualism on American culture. It does not, however, believe that individualism is overcome by simply subordinating individuals to community. Strong community requires sacrifice and generosity, and sacrifice and generosity require strong individuals. Rather than pitting individuals and community against one another, this book sees strong community and strong individuals as complementary. Individualism has certainly weakened community ties in America, but it has done so not simply by making individuals stronger and community weaker, but by weakening both. In its worst, self-absorbed forms, American individualism is a cult of individual weaknesses. It is precisely through strong forms of association that individuals realize their strength and full potential.

Scale matters. In order for the voluntary sector to be strong we need to take seriously what Wilfred McClay refers to as "proximate contexts" for democratic life and activity.[8] That is, local associations and the face-to-face environments they create depend heavily on moral habits for their success. Abstract ideas and solutions formulated in boardrooms far from real neighborhood problems frequently ignore the importance of local knowledge and the kind of obligation that exists in human-scale relationships. We recognize that it is not enough to talk about "civil society" or the "voluntary sector" in the abstract, or to make no distinctions between their national and local manifestations. Rather, we need to understand that their localized expressions matter for our moral health. Our moral vitality is formed not in a classroom or by reading books or attending conferences but by being engaged with others in solving problems, making important decisions, and finding a common purpose. And our sense of obligation is stronger the closer and more regular our contact with those in our community.

Creating conditions for moral health matters more than "moralizing." This book directs our vision to the important work of creating the conditions for moral health. This is different from preaching a particular morality. Voluntary associations are especially important in this regard. Houses of worship, grass-roots organizations formed for a publicly beneficial purpose, neighborhood associations, parental volunteer organizations in schools, inner-city youth programs, and numerous other voluntary associations create the settings in which the cultivation of moral habits is likely, though not guaranteed. Moral reinvigoration can never be guaranteed, but we can create environments that make it more or less probable. Regardless of which set of moral beliefs we might preach, our engagement in associations usually requires that we practice the moral habits most of us already cherish. It is difficult to be involved in associations without practicing various forms of generosity, fairness, mutual assistance, and the like. Thus an enriched set of options in the voluntary sector will increase the likelihood of a strengthened moral fabric in America. Creating the conditions for moral health means that we spend our efforts not on trying to guarantee (by force) adherence to a set of moral principles, but on putting into place various sets of relationships and activities that make the practice of moral habits something more common tomorrow than we find today.

Not all habits are equal. Some are good for us, others are not. Just as the neglect of certain physical habits denigrates our physical health and produces social costs, so does the neglect of moral habits have negative social consequences. We spend billions of taxpayer dollars annually treating forms of diabetes that result from poor eating and exercise habits, and we spend enormous amounts of money treating the effects of smoking every year. These costs, which we incur due to poor health habits, have become fairly well known, and very few "physical relativists" object to their portrayal as "bad" or at least "unhealthy."

Moral relativists, on the other hand, are far less likely to accept the notion that neglecting moral habits creates costs that all of us bear. But what are we to make of increasing debt loads that signal a lack of restraint among a culture of consumers? Or what do we make of the rising number of lawsuits that signal a lack of reciprocity among citizens? Or what do we make of the fatherlessness in our culture that signals an alarming lack of sacrifice on the part of parents for the sake of their children? These and other weaknesses in our social fabric carry costs that, in one way or another, affect us all.

The Order of This Book

Part one addresses the tension that currently exists in American society between a culturally entrenched individualism that threatens our moral vitality on the one hand and promising signs of civic renewal on the other. Individualism is more than simple self-interest; rather, it manifests itself in a general neglect of others and is produced by a combination of forces, from the impersonal nature of important institutions to the alienation of legitimate forms of moral authority. But the art of civic renewal and association is also deeply rooted in America, and it is making a bold comeback.

Part two looks at the vital role that voluntary associations play for government and market activity. Americans have long understood that a strong political and commercial order is based upon the habits of citizenship—and that these habits are formed primarily outside of both government and market activity. Voluntary associations, as incubators of public virtue, play an important role in humanizing business as well as social life.

Part three concretely addresses the topic of moral habits and their public significance. After decades of pretending that values could be kept neutral, Americans are now more readily recognizing that some modes of behavior serve the public good in obvious ways while others do not. Part three speaks frankly about what some of these behaviors are and what can be done to encourage them.

Notes

1. Gertrude Himmelfarb, "Democratic Remedies for Democratic Disorders," *Public Interest* (Spring 1998): 5.

2. Edward Shils, *The Virtue of Civility: Selected Essays on Liberalism, Tradition, and Civil Society* (Indianapolis: Liberty Fund, 1997), 335, 338.

3. Stephen Carter, *Civility: Manners, Morals, and the Etiquette of Democracy* (New York: Basic Books, 1998), 11.

4. Carter, *Civility*, 11.

5. Edmund Burke, *Reflections on the Revolution in France*, ed. J. C. D. Clark (Stanford: Stanford University Press, 2000), 202.

6. Jean Bethke Elshtain, "Not a Cure-All: Civil Society Creates Citizens, It Does Not Solve Problems," in *Community Works: The Revival of Civil Society in America*, ed. E. J. Dionne (Washington, D. C. : Brookings, 1998), 28.

7. Elshtain, "Not a Cure-All," 29.

8. Wilfred McClay, "The Soul of Man Under Federalism," *First Things* 64 (June-July, 1996): 23.

PART ONE

THE PROMISE OF SOCIAL RENAISSANCE

Chapter One

The Coming Social Renaissance
Restoring America's Civic and Moral Creed

Don Eberly

America's Civic Vitality

The most important development at the beginning of the twenty-first century was the rediscovery of the nongovernmental sector of civil society, or as some call it, the voluntary or social sector. If the twentieth century was about the neglect, and even the systematic destruction of civil society through statist ideologies and destructive cultural influences, the twenty-first century may represent the era of its restoration.[1]

After decades of neglect, Americans are rediscovering that the social sector—consisting of families, neighborhoods, voluntary associations, and an endless variety of civic enterprises—is an essential and irreplaceable part of our democratic experiment. This sector performs thousands of essential functions in communities every day, from compassionate neighborly care, to maintaining public order and cleanliness, to meeting the recreational and social needs of residents.

Still more important than the practical functions of civil society is the role this sector plays in cultivating citizenship and generating values. Public in nature, though not governmental, the social sector provides public "space" where people learn through practice such essential democratic habits as trust, collaboration, and compromise.

Few things are more important to America's social order than the dynamic role voluntary associations and private charities have played in creating a stronger society. This social sector represents the most dynamic and unique force within the American system.

For one, it represents a peculiarly American channel for social action and moral transformation. Many of the great social reform movements in history, whether centering on moral uplift, justice for women and children, or the eradication of poverty and suffering, were orchestrated by voluntary associations. At various periods in the nineteenth century, America witnessed an explosion in civic initiative which led to the creation of many of the charities that serve to this day.

The story of America's wide network of voluntary associations and activities has long been considered a principal source of America's distinctiveness and strength, as any number of foreign observers have noted over the course of American history. Few appreciate just how inseparable this civic vitality is from other American distinctions, such as the tradition of limited government and the separation of church and state. Historically in America, if civic work was to be done, it was to be done largely by individuals, not predominantly by government, and by an empowered religious laity, not merely by the ordained clergymen of an official church who are hired to do this kind of thing, as was common in Europe.

In other words, civil society is part and parcel of who we are. It is a central feature of our history, a history which has been periodically renewed and appears to be entering a period of rebirth again in the early stages of the twenty-first century.

Evidence of Civic Renaissance

Fortunately, there are many signs at the beginning of the twenty-first century that the social sector is coming alive again, witnessed especially by a fresh outpouring of social entrepreneurship and civic reinvention. Increasingly, there is evidence of yet another fresh wave of charitable and civic initiative emerging to deliver an array of important goods, from crime watches to programs for poor youth to supplying food and shelter services for the hungry and homeless. There are five reasons why America may be on the verge of a social revival of Tocquevillian dimensions.

Lost Faith in Centralization. The first factor is the collapse of confidence in centralized systems of government, especially the welfare state as it has evolved since the New Deal, which is producing strong pressure for the devolution of policy, not merely downward toward local units of government, but outward toward nongovernmental institutions in the community.

The relationship between civil society and the state is complex. While it is true that these sectors have always overlapped to some extent, the relationship between civil society and government has increasingly been characterized by competition and conflict, to the detriment of civil society. Civil society, with its quiet, voluntary ways, is no match for the taxing and regulating powers of a central state. Few doubt that the welfare state has supplanted private civic initiative to some extent. The debate is over the extent to which that displacement has occurred, and what should be done to revive civil society once it has been weakened.

The drive against the central welfare state in recent years has been driven by much more than concern over rising costs. It has been fueled by a desire to push back against the bureaucratization of America. The encroachment of trained and pedigreed "social service professionals" into nearly every corner of our society suffocates citizenship and discourages local nonprofessional care givers from getting involved in healing and renewing the lives of the poor.

What the return of interest in the social sector reflects is a repudiation of twentieth-century ideologies premised on grandiose dreams of national community and a loss of support for large, secular megastructures. What people long for today are real communities—local, particular, cohesive—as a bulwark against the uprooting forces of modernity and its impersonal structures.

The Quest for Values. The second factor is the search for values that registers consistently in public opinion polls. It is in communities, not through the large bureaucratic structures of modern society, where values must be recovered. This fits with a public which harbors a desire to see values renewed, but which is very doubtful that the work of moral renewal should be undertaken mostly by the state. In fact, it is the failure of society and culture to maintain ethical norms that causes many to turn to the state. As Peter Berger and Richard John Neuhaus have stated, "Mediating structures are the value-generating, value-maintaining agencies in society. Without them, values become another function of the megastructures, most notably the state."[2]

Much is lost when the mediating structures of neighborhood and family are bypassed and modern society becomes organized entirely around either the mechanism of the market or the state. For one, individuals are encouraged to see themselves, not as citizens of communities but as self-interested, rights-bearing consumers, a mentality which has contributed powerfully to the rise of modern individualism and social fragmentation.

Increased Volume of Volunteers. The third factor that points to the possibility of civic renewal is the renewed interest in volunteerism that is taking place across the entire age spectrum. America's retired population is healthier, more prosperous, and probably more active than any ever. Almost 110 million Americans now volunteer, averaging 3.5 hours per week, and that is likely to grow.

The twenty-first century, according to forecasters, will yield a significant increase in volunteering by the retired and semiretired, filling such essential roles as mentoring and serving in local charities. A new phenomenon among middle-agers called "half-timers" is taking shape in which entrepreneurs who have achieved financial success are trading in "money for meaning," according to the movement's leader, Texas entrepreneur Bob Buford. Numerous indicators of increased civic activism are also showing up on college campuses and among America's youth.

Inherited Wealth. Fourth, we are about to witness the largest intergenerational transfer of human wealth in history. Not only have the "baby boomers" created enormous amounts of new wealth, but for decades to come, they and their children will be the inheritors of the trillions of dollars represented by their parent's wealth.

The first five decades of the twenty-first century will see a transfer of at least $41 trillion. The availability of these two forms of wealth—new wealth and inherited wealth—will make unprecedented resources available for charitable investment. John Havens and Paul Schervish, the leading commentators on this phenomenon, estimate that $6 trillion will be available for charitable purposes between 1998 and 2052 as a result of this inherited wealth.[3]

These factors taken together are yielding predictions of a new "golden age of philanthropy." "Giving by Americans, individually and institutionally, is poised to grow at an astounding rate," predicts John Walters.[4] And that giving will likely generate new social ventures, ones which are results-oriented and highly entrepreneurial, just like the entrepreneurs who created the wealth in the first place. The new rich view civic endeavors much as they view venture-capital firms; they think in terms of "giving away money in the same way they made it—through small, flexible institutions, very focused, outcome-driven."[5]

The Social Sector as an Arena of Effective Action. Fifth, the social sector has suddenly taken on new credibility because it is perceived to be an arena of effective public action.

Poll after poll reveals that large majorities of the American people see conventional political action as synonymous with gridlock, excessive self-interest, and ineffectiveness. By contrast, many are searching for the means to improve society outside of conventional political involvement and are turning to the social sector, which is controlled by citizens and generally free of partisan taint.

Many observers have concluded that political disengagement must surely signal public indifference, but in reality, much of the passion and vision that was once directed toward political action is now frequently directed toward civic renewal. The driving impulse of these social sector initiatives is neither political power nor economic profit, but rather social improvement.

A new generation of civic activists is discovering the workings of social or civic capitalism. Chris Gates of the National Civic League describes it as turning from capital "P" politics to small "p" politics, focusing on small, local, and results-oriented forms of civic involvement. Says philanthropic expert John Walters, the world of private philanthropy is about to become "the most dynamic growth sector of domestic American life."[6]

The social sector increasingly has its own distinct identity, language, and dynamics. In many respects, the social sector is its own economy, with its own institutions, offering careers to a growing percentage of the nation's workforce. Management guru Peter Drucker reports that over 800,000 new nonprofits have been created over the past thirty years. This trend has not slowed. The IRS reports that 45,000 new charities were created in 2000 alone.[7] Drucker states "the growth sector of a developed society in the twenty-first century is mostly unlikely to be business."[8]

Reflecting this trend is the growing number of professional schools that are providing degrees in nonprofit management and research into the workings of the nonprofit sector. Drucker calls for "principled, theory-based management" of this emerging social sector. Successful leadership in this sector, he says, could yield major results on the enormous problems facing the world.[9]

Also contributing to the rise of interest in the social sector is an explosion of academic research from across numerous social science fields focusing on the state of "social capital" in America. Magazines, journals, and newsletters serving the nonprofit sector are proliferating.

Interest in reviving the social sector has increasingly affected public debate. New terms, like "compassionate conservative," "communitarian," and the "civil society movement" have entered the public vernacular. Political consultant Dick Morris captures the political ramifications of the contest of ideas in this emerging field this way: "Democrats own the public sector; Republicans own the private sector. But the voluntary sector—where the action is — is up for grabs. The party that makes the voluntary sector its own will acquire a lock on America's conscience." A more scholarly source, Michael Novak, the eminent American Enterprise Institute author, made a similar observation: "The American political party that best gives life and breath and amplitude to civil society will not only thrive in the twenty-first century. It will win popular gratitude and it will govern."

The recent embrace of a "civil society model" in public policy, which evaluates the success of policies in light of their impact on communities and which, to the greatest degree possible, relies on civic institutions to achieve public goods, is a welcome trend. In the end, more is at stake than the replacement of monopolistic government services with a pluralistic system of social service delivery, as vital as that is. These local civic networks become the incubators of democratic citizenship and habits. They are where we learn neighborly regard, practical civic problem-solving, and democratic values.

Civic Renewal and Moral Renewal

Ever since the term "civil society" entered the public debate in the mid-1990s, even informed observers have been confused over what exactly it means and where it is leading us. Although the concept of civil society has had a rich history in Western thought, it had fallen out of use until very recently.

The boundaries of the term are flexible, but everyone acknowledges that at a minimum they encompass the entire web of voluntary associations that dot our social landscape: families, neighborhoods, civic associations, charitable enterprises, and local networks of a thousand kinds. For some of us, civil society also embraces our national public philosophy and our culture—in other words, all of those intangible values and beliefs upon which democracy rests, as well as those very tangible institutions in which they are cultivated and sustained.

Voluntary associations are often referred to as "mediating structures" because they stand as a buffer between the individual and the large impersonal structures of the state and the economic market. Civil society is not an economic sphere where self-interested persons compete for advantage, nor is it generally understood as part of the political sphere where individuals and factions gather to gain power. Rather, civil society is a social sector where individuals are drawn together into horizontal relationships of trust and collaboration.

The weaker this layer of civic association, the stronger the vertical relationship of the individual and the state becomes—a relationship characterized not by voluntary action and cooperation, but by power, authority, and dependence. When civil society atrophies, the individual is left more and more isolated in a politicized and conflicted society in which all roads lead to the lawyer's office, to the courts, and to social agencies, which are increasingly called upon to exercise a custodial function over vulnerable individuals and fragile families.

The institutions of civil society are important, not only because they perform innumerable functions in countless locations every day, but also because they generate individual character and democratic habits. Through these institutions and networks, we become socialized as adult citizens, capable of being helpful, trustful, and respectful. Not surprisingly, many political theorists, most notably Alexis de Tocqueville, saw them as the basis of American greatness. If they weakened, he believed, American democracy would be imperiled.

No foreign observer deserves more credit for having bequeathed to us the capacity to understand the roots and requirements of our own democracy than Tocqueville. The civil society debate of the 1990s cannot be understood apart from the basic questions and doubts that Tocqueville injected into our collective consciousness during the mid-nineteenth century. Tocqueville was amazed by the power and vitality of American democracy, but was equally convinced that it contained seeds of its own corruption. Indeed, if there is any single concern that has animated today's civil society movement, it is the fear that American democracy has developed weaknesses.

But this discussion of civil society has its skeptics, who suspect the idea is vague and evasive, glossing over deeper and important ideological differences— perhaps intentionally. Some on the left has seen it as code for reaction, nostalgia, and conformity. Some on the right have seen it as perhaps too unaffirming of free markets and of the hard work of dismantling the welfare state and remoralizing the culture. Some critics complain that the entire civil society debate appears superficial and sentimental, offering inspiring themes but no concrete program for policymakers.

Perhaps the moment has arrived for a fresh evaluation. We would do well to follow the lead of two major national study groups that labored quietly at the end of the 1990s to address these issues of civil society and civic renewal. They regularly met, debated, sifted through research and polling data, and tried to make sense of all of the issues that the civil society debate has brought to the forefront: the loss of trust, the decline of civic participation, the weakening of core social institutions, and the erosion of public morality.

These two commissions were led by heavyweights and loaded with ideologically diverse scholars and public advocates of civic revival. One was the Pew-funded National Commission on Civic Renewal, cochaired by former U.S. Secretary of Education William Bennett and former U.S. Senator Sam Nunn, and directed by William Galston, a former policy adviser to President Clinton and arguably the nation's leading civil-society intellectual. The other commission was the Council on Civil Society, sponsored jointly by the University of Chicago Divinity School and the Institute for American Values, and cochaired by Jean Elshtain, the prolific author and commentator, and David Blankenhorn, who is quickly emerging as one of the nation's most creative and formidable cultural reformers.

Both commissions released reports, which have circulated around the country and filled the nation's airwaves with debate. In many ways, the commissions were similar and addressed overlapping concerns. Each took as its starting point what I call the Paradox of American Progress: the dismaying fact that the United States is the world's undisputed military, economic, and technological leader, yet also leads the world in many categories of social pathology.

Each report confronts the myth that economic progress assures widespread social progress. Each emphasizes the importance of renewing the family, especially curbing divorce and out-of-wedlock childbearing. Each strongly decries the state of America's media and entertainment culture. Each laments a possible decline in the civic spirit and its attendant virtues of civic trust and cooperation. Each speaks to the erosion of common moral norms and the rise of a corrupted form of individualism. And each offers a panoply of proposals for cleaning up the culture, fixing our institutions, and reinvigorating our public life.

Although there are many similarities in the reports, they reflect two diverging streams of argument in the civil society debate with significantly different priorities. One wing seems mostly concerned about the civic life of the nation, the other mostly about the nation's culture and moral underpinnings.

The first wing was drawn into the debate through the provocative work of Harvard scholar Robert Putnam, especially his famous essay "Bowling Alone," in which he questioned whether Americans are still civic joiners. Putnam offered evidence—since widely challenged—that Americans were withdrawing from many mainstream civic associations and were essentially becoming isolated. Although the National Commission on Civic Renewal report addressed a wide range of moral and cultural topics as well as civic ones, its title, "A Nation of Spectators: How Civic Disengagement Weakens America and What We Can Do About It," places it squarely in the Putnam camp.

This wing of the civil society movement, which I call civic revivalists, appears to be interested mostly in promoting public work by individuals. This usually means civic work in furtherance of fairly conventional governmental objectives. Putnam's original research, which focused on regional governments in Italy, found that public support for government was far stronger when surrounded by strong civic communities. In other words, this group wants civic recovery, among other things, to temper the public's recent repudiation of government activism by splicing in an emphasis on civic localism. The overriding objective, in any event, is promoting civic works, not inspiring a renewal of ethics or cultural values.

One senses in this group a significant amount of discomfort with talk of morality, especially religion. Deliberations at the National Commission on Civic Renewal polarized repeatedly over the question of whether our society's deficits are mostly civic or mostly moral. Interestingly, although the final report was very balanced and nuanced, both William Bennett and Sam Nunn were decidedly in the cultural camp. A significant contingent of the civic restorationists responded with indignation over the possibility that the new civic conversation in America might include talk of moral values.

Civil society intellectuals of this school frequently go overboard in attempting to narrow the boundaries of debate around civic issues. I recently shared a platform with Benjamin Barber, a noted scholar from this camp, who stated emphatically, "What we don't need is moral character, but civic character. Our aim is democratic citizens; not the moral man." He added, "A society does not need moral truths; we need to live together."

Notice that he sought to equate moral truths with an implied threat of intolerance or moral majoritarianism. Barber's remarks are something of a bellwether of the philosophical impoverishment that still guides this debate in many quarters. His side allows that religion deserves a stronger voice in the public square, because to insist otherwise is to marginalize it, but it resists the notion that our democratic experiment is grounded in moral truth or transcendence of even the thinnest kind. What is sufficient for a democracy, they say, is civic character, or, in other words, a quickness to join. This is essentially civic secularism, and it largely misses the point.

If the public today has any preference for the basis of a reevaluation of American society, it points decidedly in the direction of moral values. According to Daniel Yankelovich, "Public distress about the state of our social morality has reached nearly universal proportions: 87 percent of the public fear that something is fundamentally wrong with America's moral condition." Sixty-seven percent of Americans believe their country is in a long-term moral decline. By a margin of 59 percent to 27 percent, Americans believe that "lack of morality" is a greater problem in the United States than "lack of economic opportunity."

The civic character argument is not unimportant: It represents a new point of potential convergence in our nation's public life. For example, politicians of both parties show a growing interest in empowering community-based charities. This is constructive as far as it goes, but it offers thin gruel for a nation looking for deeper transformation. How, one must ask, do gentle appeals to civic-mindedness help curb teen pregnancy, confront the crack epidemic, stop playground shootings, slow the vulgarization of American culture, or reverse the complete demoralization of our schools?

The public is quite clear on this. If some civic renewal advocates are dismayed by the discussion of moral reformation, many others see admonitions of civic engagement as inadequate and misplaced. The editors of my hometown newspaper scoffed at the Bennett-Nunn commission's suggestion that there's a failure of civic spirit, a response probably typical of many other small towns. Local folks in my central Pennsylvanian town, who like me are steeped in the gentle communitarianism of the Anabaptists or "plain people" of the area, simply do not understand what the fuss about civic decline is all about.

The habit of being "our brother's keeper" is deeply ingrained where I come from. An early morning fire recently destroyed the bedroom of a local farmhouse, leaving smoke damage throughout the entire dwelling. By sundown, fifty or so local volunteers—neighbors and relatives who showed up spontaneously, without prompting or moral admonishments by outsiders—had rid the house of every trace of smoke damage.

These folks would hoot at the thought that we Americans lack civic commitment. What really leaves them astonished is the sense of powerlessness they feel as they watch the bottom fall out of the nation's moral life, especially evidenced in the popular culture. As inconceivable as it is for these folks to not show up when the tragedy of fire or flood strikes, so, too, is the idea that our society would tolerate the loss of innocence in an increasingly toxic culture, wink at the problem of family collapse, and watch diffidently as unmarried mothers give birth to more than one-third of American children. How, they ask, can national leaders think that the civic spirit can be recaptured when we refuse to cultivate conscience among the young. Most importantly, they wonder, how can a nation advance by placing its faith in prosperity and civic participation alone.

The Council on Civil Society, which took this concern essentially as its starting point, stated its challenge boldly in the report's title: "A Call to Civil Society: Why Democracy Needs Moral Truths." "Our main challenge," it stated, "is to rediscover the existence of transmittable moral truth." Gently chiding those who argue that all we need is to spend more time volunteering, the report spotlighted "a deeper problem." American civic institutions are declining, it said, "because the moral ideas that fueled and formed them are losing their power to shape our behavior and unite us." "This weakening," it continued, "is closely connected to a range of social problems, from listless voting patterns to fragmenting families, from the coarsening of popular culture to expanding economic inequality."

The Council on Civil Society also issued a clarion call for civic renewal, but it concluded that America's civic crisis is primarily philosophical and moral. "Why would anyone want to participate in civic life in the first place? Why work to relieve suffering or achieve justice? Why tolerate dissent, why seek to persuade rather than overpower and rule? Even the most elementary civic act, such as voting, cannot be explained merely in terms of rational self-interest." The report argued that "the qualities necessary for self-governance are the results of certain moral ideas about the human person and the nature of the good life," and when the moral grounds of our existence is ignored, "all that is left is power."

A national consensus is beginning to emerge on certain key public concerns such as family disintegration and out-of-wedlock childbearing. Moreover, notwithstanding the reservations of some, religion is likely to have a stronger voice in the public square, both as a legitimate wellspring of personal values and as perhaps the richest source of renewed social capital in communities. It means that civil society is going to be a powerful place for people to gather and work, in many cases transcending politics and ideology.

Most will rejoice to know that a majority of Americans now acknowledge that government, and especially the central government, may never again be embraced as the engine that drives American social progress, even though it will continue to carry heavy responsibilities in a host of areas. In the arena of civil society, a far more dynamic form of citizenship is being reborn, not one that concerns itself exclusively with casting a vote so that action can be taken in some distant legislature, but one that concerns itself with the improvement of living conditions in our neighborhoods.

In political terms, this means that a public philosophy is emerging that attempts to summon Americans toward greater and higher purposes than are usually invoked by simple appeals to self-interest and the economic bottom line. The values of citizenship, sacrifice, service to others, and the ethic of cooperation will once more gain strength.

The emergence of civil society as a framework for progress means that simplistic reliance on either the state or the market as mechanisms for social improvement will give way to deepening interest in creative ways to expand the social sector. The people long for relationships that last, human exchange that is trustworthy, institutions that function, and civic communities that rely firmly on life-enhancing values.

The stage is set for a far more promising and perhaps unexpected debate. That debate will center on the moral versus civic requirements of American citizenship. Was our constitution written for a moral and religious people, or was that merely a quaint sentiment which dominated during less enlightened times when we had fewer social protections against the risk of bad behavior? Will the recovery of civic character get us through the social storm, or will the renewal of our democratic experiment require more? This, it seems, is the question.

Notes

1. A portion of the present chapter appeared as "Civic Renewal vs. Moral Renewal," *Policy Review* 91 (September-October 1998). Permission to reproduce the article in its present modified form has been generously granted by the Heritage Foundation.

2. Peter L. Berger and Richard John Neuhaus, *To Empower People: The Role of Mediating Structures in Public Policy* (Washington, D.C.: American Enterprise Institute, 1977), 2.

3. John J. Havens and Paul G. Schervish, *Millionaires and the Millennium: New Estimates of the Forthcoming Wealth Transfer and the Prospects for a Golden Age of Philanthropy* (Boston: Social Welfare Research Institute, 1999), 1.

4. John P. Walters, "The Coming Philanthropic Explosion," *Philanthropy* (Winter 1997): 2.

5. David Ignatius, "How To Give Away Mountains of Money," *Washington Post*, January 17, 1999, B7.

6. Walters, "Philanthropic Explosion," 2.

7. Reshma Memon Yaqub, "A Gift for Giving," *Worth* (December 2001).

8. Peter F. Drucker, "Management's New Paradigms," *Forbes* (October 5, 1998): 156.

9. Drucker, "Management's New Paradigms," 158.

Chapter Two

Toward a Human Scale
Making the World Work at the Street Level

Ryan Streeter

Whether one is a liberal or a conservative in today's terms usually depends on two things: first, one's view of how centralized and controlling government should be, and second, how free business and investment should be. The significance that a person attaches to each of these two elements generally determines whether he or she is a free market conservative, a social conservative, a New Democrat, a good old liberal, or something else.

American political history is no doubt a history about the proper role and scope of government and commerce. The birth of our nation is a drama rooted in the view that there are certain things governments simply ought not be able to do, especially in the areas of commerce and taxation. Our constitutional beginnings are a story about how we decided to balance a national government with robust and independent states. At the core of this history is the question about how much control the federal government should have over the affairs of private citizens and how extensive it needs to be to exercise that control.

But the centralization of government and the freedom of the market are only a part of the story. There is a compelling, often untold, story about the size of our society's institutions themselves and what they have come to mean for our well-being and happiness. This story has had an immeasurable effect on the way we live, the way we conceive of ourselves as citizens, and the way we contribute to the health of society. It is a story about the relative loss of a human scale to our everyday life.

A Disquieting History

The second half of the nineteenth century began a trend toward what I call BIG: *bureaucratic individualizing gigantism.* Governments in Europe and America began to consolidate and centralize their operations in substantial ways. Business in America began to see the merits of centralized operations and began to build the bureaucratic organizations that we associate with the industrial era. Large institutions became home to mass collections of individuals, whose community associations grew to be of secondary, rather than primary, importance.

Governmental centralization became the norm in America in the half-century following the Civil War. Progressivism capitalized on the national identity that emerged in the half-century after the war and built a centralized governmental culture in Washington, D.C. The trend did not exist in the United States alone. Europe, it might be said, experienced the darker side of consolidation as one nation after another, in the words of Gordon Craig, abandoned the "creeds of liberalism" still prevalent in the 1850s—such as individual liberty, competition, suspicion of big government—in favor of mass consolidation, "for this was the age of trusts, monopolies, and cartels."[1]

Business life reinforced this trend. Advances in production technology during this time facilitated the mass distribution of goods through railroad networks that, combined with communication advances, created unprecedented national and international markets for those goods. Increasingly, the largest companies began capturing greater market share and thus created layers of middle managers to effectively organize their massive operations.[2]

Not long after this trend toward centralization began, supplemental forces made it stronger. For instance, with current revenues of $714 million, the federal government implemented an income tax in 1913 that enabled it to grow in an unprecedented way. By 1917, revenues passed the billion dollar mark for the first time and reached $5.1 billion by 1919. With the introduction of the withholding tax on wages in 1943, revenues jumped from $24 billion to $43.7 billion in one year and reached $69.6 billion ten years later. These and other developments enabled our nation to operate successfully in the new world of the twentieth century. They have made possible many good things.

They have also made possible mass-scale government operations by growing and expanding beyond the federal government's original chief functions of regulating commerce, providing a common defense, and handling foreign affairs. Our huge governmental infrastructure made it less necessary for average citizens to engage in their local governments and associations for help, direction, and services. Certainly, there existed weaknesses and inequities in local life that mass-scale government intervention addressed. It cannot be overstated, however, just how underappreciated this shift toward large-scale institutions is today.

Americans routinely offer lamentations about "big government," which they will from time to time carry to extremes, but in general, most of us are far more accustomed to, and perhaps even dependent upon, big government than we realize. As R. Shep Melnick has astutely observed, we rail against big government in one survey but are strangely comfortable in our roles as passive consumers of its goods in another. While "loathing bureaucracy in the abstract," Americans "report favorable opinions of agencies with which they have had contact. Americans, it seems, can't live with big government—and can't live without it."[3]

A mass-scale society has also continued to grow through the centralization of businesses in America, which has made BIG an economic way of life. Large factories, often situated on water, became symbols of progress in the industrial era, despite their impersonal and inhumane qualities. Skyscrapers, which are truly feats of human ingenuity and imagination, soon became the avatars of corporate success and prosperity—despite the historically unique, if not odd, work environment they create in which people are housed vertically from 8:00 a.m. to 5:00 p.m. completely separated from the community in which everything else in their lives occur. The first works of what we now call business management theory, following the example set by Frederick Winslow Taylor's *The Principles of Scientific Management* in 1911, prescribed bureaucratic, segmented, hierarchical organizations in order to maximize productivity and profit.

As cities became increasingly congested and expensive, corporations and people left their vertical lifestyles in favor of the horizontal lifestyle of the suburbs, where chopping up life into large-scale sections has been perfected. Fifty percent of all Americans live in suburbs today, where they work in office parks, shop in strip malls, live in housing developments, and send their children to huge schools where principals are lucky to know half of the students' names—with virtually no town center or public space where commerce and house, park and store intersect. This kind of categorized living is supported by law: most zoning ordinances segregate land by its use, making it illegal to build the kind of integrated communities that many idealize (think of Alexandria, Virginia, or a New England town) for their mix of public, commercial, and residential uses.[4]

Also, suburban—and even urban—living is becoming a highly segregated way of life. There are 20,000 gated housing developments in the United States—almost all of which have been built since 1980. These communities "focus inward, emphasizing private over public space" in an extreme way.[5] We have not yet even begun to ask whether or not this should make us uncomfortable, or what the social effects on larger metropolitan areas are.

Living with BIG

These trends throughout the twentieth century made town and village, community and neighborhood, seem outdated. Local associations were viewed for most of the century as inefficient symbols of a past that should be left behind. And, as a number of astute observers have noted, a decline in participation in community associations signals an increase in individualizing forces—namely, more and more people simply become individuals in and amidst large, impersonal institutions without feeling a part of a smaller, more personal community.

The trouble with these trends is not "big government," but that the larger part of our society as a whole lacks a human scale—from the places we live to the places we shop to the places we work to how we live. Public administrations, school boards, corporate boards, and now even nonprofit membership groups—the most effective of which have become highly sophisticated lobbying machines based in Washington, D.C., as Robert Putnam has shown—seem far away and inaccessible to most Americans.[6] We do not know how to engage these institutions without high-level connections. We cannot reach human beings on their phones, or if we can, they usually transfer us to someone else who does not know how to answer our question (and who usually transfers us again).

More ominously, it is difficult to separate the madness of loners with an appetite for violence from the absence of well-rounded, human-scale association in their own lives. Should we be surprised that the majority of murderers at our nation's schoolhouses have been loners, disconnected from healthy forms of community? Aristotle wrote nearly 2,500 years ago that a creature who has no need of social interaction "must be either a beast or a god" but could not be part of a human community.[7] For to be human is to be fit for—and in need of—engagement with others. We are by nature creatures who derive happiness not only by feeling accepted in a caring community but also by contributing to it.

Well-rounded communities also provide an enhanced "village eye" that can spot abnormal or questionable behavior more quickly. While this can degenerate into clannishness or forms of social bigotry, communities whose members are interconnected and share expressed communal concerns can more easily enforce healthy norms and spot violators of those norms before it is too late. This is simply the way that a healthy society operates. As communitarian Amitai Etzioni writes, when communities relegate their responsibilities to enforce basic decent behavior to the state, the larger society "is in a deep moral crisis."[8]

Because we have lost so many vestiges of human scale in our core practices and institutions, it is harder for us to act like citizens. What is worse, we often do not see this as a problem—or if we do, we likely do not see how our way of life keeps us from doing much about it. We remain a nation of great generosity, evidenced by our record-level philanthropic and volunteer activity, but we also have become a nation of disengagement. We do less for others, we trust each other less, and we define citizenship by tax payments and Social Security numbers.[9] This sounds a lot like life at the mall, where instead of Social Security cards we offer credit cards as proof of our right to be there. Both are consumer, not citizen, cultures.

I suggest that BIG has actually won—at least for now. It has become our predominant way of life, even after the 1990s in which we tried to convince ourselves that our "new economy" and "reinvented governments" have knocked down the walls of BIG culture. This claim, to be sure, flies in the face of conventional wisdom. But consider the following:

More and more Americans are working for large firms, and the number of large firms themselves is increasing dramatically. The number of Americans working for companies with more than 500 employees increased by 32.9 percent between 1988 and 1998, compared to 14.9 percent among those with fewer than 500 employees (and among these, the growth happened mostly in the larger firms). The number of business establishments with fewer than 500 employees grew by 12.9 percent during this time, compared to 35.3 percent for 500-plus employee companies. Americans working for large companies now account for almost half (49.1 percent) of the entire labor force.[10] This is not to suggest that large corporations cannot provide subenvironments approximating the human scale for their employees; however, it is a sign that increasing numbers of Americans are working more like units than members of an enterprise.

Corporate mergers and acquisitions grew explosively in the past decade. Between 1992 and 1997, the total transaction value of this activity increased six-fold to more than $1 trillion. In 1998 alone there were twenty-four bank consolidation deals worth more than $500 million apiece, and seventeen banks disappeared from the list of the largest 100 banks as a result of mergers. Following merger and acquisition activity, customer satisfaction usually drops significantly as people find themselves poorly served by new layers of organization.[11]

Federal outlays continue to account for nearly one-fifth of America's gross domestic product. Though it is presently on a downward track (largely because of the recent economic expansion of the 1990s), federal outlays considered as a percentage of America's gross domestic product have hovered around 20 percent since the 1960s.[12]

Federal spending grows even during a time of "reinvention" and downsizing. Between 1992 and 1999, when the Clinton administration launched an aggressive initiative to "reinvent" government, the number of federal employees was cut by 5 percent. However, federal spending increased 29.5 percent.[13] Expensive government programs continued to grow; there were simply fewer people to manage them.

Americans are moving to large cities but living farther apart. Nearly half of all Americans live in 243 cities that have populations greater than 100,000. But unlike the traditional high-density city, today's fastest growing are untraditional lower-density places. In fact, of the fastest growing 75 cities with more than 100,000 residents, only one (Houston) had more than one million residents in 1990. In other words, the older large cities such as New York, Chicago, Los Angeles, and Philadelphia are growing much more slowly (or negatively, in Philadelphia's case) as Americans favor less dense living arrangements in "horizontal cities" that do not offer the high-density residential and commercial districts typical of older cities. Furthermore, in 1980, two-thirds of American jobs were in the lower-density suburbs, compared to four-fifths today. While there is no necessary correlation between BIG culture and low-density "horizontal cities," suburban single-use zoning and the lack of shared public space combine with lower-density housing and working environments to foster the "individualizing" aspect of BIG perhaps more than anything.

The past 150 years have been about more than how centralized government is and how free the market is. It has been about BIG. And it is far less clear in BIG's case what makes one a liberal or conservative. BIG is a way of life that members of both sides of the ideological divide embrace and that most Americans have grown used to.

But even though BIG has become our way of life, that does not mean we like it. The last two to three decades of the twentieth century in the United States witnessed a booming interest in community, social capital, and civil society. A "community industry" arose. It became acceptable to refer to oneself as a "communitarian," academics began to conduct elaborate investigations into "social capital," government programs seemed to require anything to be "community-based" if it was to receive funding, the numbers of locally based community development corporations grew, and someone can now call him or herself a "new urbanist" and be taken seriously as one who has a legitimate preference for mixed-use, walkable communities. All of these developments can be viewed as a collective cry for a human scale in the face of BIG.

It is important, I believe, that we look seriously at the realities of human scale. And it is important that we go beyond nostalgic, wistful conversations about community to hard-nosed debate about human scale, what it means, and what kinds of costs society incurs when we neglect it. The trouble with much of America's fascination with community is precisely its lack of a concrete understanding of human scale. "Community" is often expressed as a pleasant add-on to American individualism. Life that respects a human scale is more fundamental than that, and it calls the American way of life to its higher self and fullest potential.

Putting the Human Back on the Scale

When we conceive of the past one hundred fifty years as BIG's assault on human scale, we are able to look at society beyond the distinctions of "left" and "right." Advocates of BIG have had stark proponents on the left and the right. Progressives and Great Society enthusiasts were enamored with a BIG government, while industrialists, corporate moguls, and bankers wanted BIG capitalism. All have contributed to a society where our fundamental modes of life are routinely defined by BIG rather than the human-scale associations from which life derives most of its meaning for most people.

The prophets of human-scale institutions have come from across the political spectrum as well. For instance, the conservatism of Robert Nisbet, whose *The Quest for Community* (1953) pointed American eyes to the neglected importance of small-scale associations, is balanced by the left's Kirkpatrick Sale, whose *Human Scale* (1980) provocatively challenged the bigness of American institutions in general.[14]

The pamphlet *To Empower People* by Peter Berger and Richard John Neuhaus, argued that human-scale associations such as congregation, neighborhood, family, and voluntary association were far more important to policymakers than we had realized.[15] These "mediating structures," as they called them, place a buffer between the individual and the large institutions of everyday life. Berger and Neuhaus's work has had considerable influence.

Many have agreed that the habits of democracy—such as restraint, responsibility, sacrifice, and hard work—are not only learned in these mediating structures but enable these structures to make positive contributions to their communities. Policymakers have begun to orient much domestic policy toward "community-based" solutions precisely in order to give families, neighborhoods, faith-based organizations, and voluntary associations a more central role. Empowerment zones, community policing and prosecution initiatives, community development programs, workforce programs, ex-offender community reentry programs, and others have all made the involvement of the small platoons of democracy a necessary component of program activities.

So what are the basic principles of a human scale? What is it about human-scale communities that is good? There are two key ideas consistent throughout the literature on the topic, though there are no doubt more.

Integrated, or Holistic, Communities. Human scale refers to that which exists on a small scale, but it means more than that. Communities can be said to exist on a human scale when their various parts—physical, human, institutional—hang together as a whole for their residents. In European cities, the town square provided this kind of integration by organizing essential government, commercial, and religious institutions in one place. In the old towns of New England, as Lewis Mumford notes, the commons brought the ideal of the European square "into full flower" by serving as a true "rallying point for the community."[16]

There is less of a "center" to most Americans' experience with their communities today, which presents a challenge to citizenship. People do not regularly interact in any personal way with representatives from society's multiple sectors in a given day; most of us live in communities far too dispersed and scattered. This is a function of the way communities are organized, not a product of a municipality's large population alone.

As the famous urbanist Jane Jacobs has shown, districts within a city often create workable neighborhoods built closer to the human scale. Far from the product of romantic nostalgia (against which Jacobs sternly warns), a workable neighborhood fosters multiple uses (residential, commercial, public, recreational) while hanging together as a unity. From her studies, Jacobs very specifically claims that in the largest cities such as New York and Chicago, once a district grows beyond a mile and a half square and exceeds an average population of between 100,000 and 125,000 residents ("I know of no district larger than 200,000 which operates like a district," she says), its neighborhoods begin to deteriorate.[17] Human scale is an interplay between holistic balance and actual size.

Likewise, the provision of services exists on a human scale when they holistically address the needs of their constituents, be they employees, citizens, customers, or recipients of charitable and other public services. For instance, a neighborhood faith-based job training program is likely to concern itself with a client's child care difficulties, help with food and other resources, and spend time working through deeply personal issues. This is quite different from the stereotypical government-run public assistance offices whose job, especially before welfare and workforce reforms, was to connect a person with a particular benefit or service—and not much else. Both might be small, but the one that exists on a human scale will be the one that meets clients on a personal level and does not treat them like units to be numbered or objects to be "dealt with."

Citizen Stake in Key Institutions. Residents in human-scale communities feel connected to their basic institutions because they have a stake in determining the course those institutions take. The benefit of integrated, or holistic, communities is that it is easier for citizens to play an active role in charitable activity, make decisions affecting community enterprises and zoning decisions, participate in political forums, hire someone based on trusted referrals, and so on. Citizenship is much more than voting and paying taxes; it is bearing some portion of responsibility for the success of the community as a whole. Large-scale, fragmented communities avail themselves more easily to expert management by specialists, leaving citizen responsibility for important community decisions at a minimum.

Beyond these general ideas, literature that argues for stronger community in America usually assumes a couple of moral principles. We might term them a "morality of human scale."

First, we are social creatures. We are built for social interaction and require it for happiness. Just as no child can possibly survive without parents, we cannot survive without some degree of fellowship. We learn virtue, self-sacrifice, and a work ethic by being in relationships more than by any inborn instinct. We look to others for affirmation of what we do and will change our behavior to please others. The best political thinkers throughout the ages have recognized that social stability depends greatly upon the habits of citizenship that are learned in healthy social environments. Interestingly, our word "idiot" comes from the Greek and Latin meaning "private person"—someone with no concern for public or societal affairs.

Second, we are more greatly affected by what is immediate and nearby than by what is remote. This is natural, and it is not always a good thing. Our child's illness concerns us far more deeply than the sickness of children in faraway nations. The pleasure of getting a new entertainment center right away often makes the consumer debt we rack up purchasing it seem distant and unimportant. It is through education and experience that we begin to train our sentiments, hopefully, to care about what is far away. But it is unrealistic to think that we can ever rid ourselves of this fundamental trait to prefer the immediate to the remote. Nor would we want to. This trait has led to immeasurable good. It stands behind myriad acts of loyalty, heroism, and patriotism throughout the ages, not to mention daily acts of faithfulness by parents toward their children and citizens toward their communities.

These two principles can certainly be tested, but together they form a moral framework that challenges standard American individualism. We will care more about our communities the closer we feel to them, and we will care more about each other the more our fates, common interests, and ideals intersect. The first principle (that we are social) without the second (that we are attached to what is immediate) leaves us unsure where to start in our efforts to rehabilitate a sense of citizenship in our communities and nation. With the second, the first principle points us to a stronger engagement in the communities right where we live.

The morality of human-scale challenges individualism by shaking up our penchant for excessive personal autonomy and the complacency about the public good that usually follows. Individualism idolizes the maximization of personal autonomy. The right-leaning version of autonomy is making money, and the left-leaning version sees it as moral license. People who are a part of human-scale communities are, in a sense, forced to care about one another regardless of what they think about maximizing autonomy. Happiness considered from the framework of human scale requires relationships and investment in others. Even if someone is an individualist by creed, if he or she lives in a community aligned to a human scale, the odds are that relationships will become more and more a part of his or her sense of happiness.

But beyond an appeal to "soft issues" like relationships, does human scale matter? It would appear that it does. For instance, research indicates that secondary schools achieve the best outcomes when their student population is between 400 and 800 students. The school as a human-scale community, where the principal knows all the students' names, generates social capital and expectations that drive children to higher levels of performance. In a nation where 70 percent of high school students attend schools of more than 1,000 students, and 50 percent attend schools of more than 1,500, this should cause some concern.[18]

Large businesses that cultivate the basic characteristics of strong community in the work environment are more profitable than those that do not. The Gallup Organization has designed and tested a twelve-point scale that measures the degree to which employees have positive relationships with coworkers, are encouraged to pursue purposes they care about, find that their contribution matters to others, and a number of other indicators of human community. Companies that score higher on the scale enjoy noticeably enhanced profitability.[19]

But business by itself cannot be counted upon to be the wellspring of community and social capital. It depends on the strength of its social capital-generating institutions such as families, neighborhoods, and personal networks to engender in people the trust and basic virtues needed for business productivity and growth. Francis Fukuyama has pointed out that nations rich in social capital—such as Germany, Japan, and the United States—have been able to build large corporations because trust is needed to make large entities function hold together. Nations low in trust, on the contrary, have a difficult time creating large businesses because the spirit of mutual cooperation is absent.[20]

Robert Putnam's research into social capital levels, first in Italy and then in the United States, shows that politics, economies, neighborhoods, and individuals simply fare better wherever trust, civic interest, and citizen responsibility are strong.[21] The benefits of human scale are evident to ordinary people. Communities that operate *as communities* offer a sense of security, inspire neighborliness, and, because they consist of stronger-than-average social networks, provide expanded opportunity.

The benefits of human-scale association have also become evident to policymakers. In fact, along with the trend toward work-oriented public benefits programs, the trend toward human-scale social services is the most noteworthy development in domestic policy over the past decade. The overused moniker, "community-based," has come to apply to a range of public programs that make use of human-scale associations to more effectively deliver services.

Human-Scale Policy?

It is worth surveying several policies and initiatives that have made restoring human scale central to their design. The following list is not exhaustive but communicates just how far we have already come in changing BIG-style government programs.

Welfare reform. The old welfare system, which made direct cash payments to individuals, was replaced in 1996 by a block grant program requiring states to take responsibility for moving welfare recipients into work. This has led states to look to effective local institutions to design grassroots safety nets and supports for people trying to make the move into the world of employment. The great interest in faith-based organizations has not surprisingly been awakened in this context. A work-first welfare system requires us to look to organizations close enough and familiar enough with low-income families' diverse needs to make the move to work a successful one.

Workforce reform. In 1998, Congress passed a law consolidating a plethora of federal job training programs into a single initiative. States were required to devolve responsibility for job training to regional workforce boards, half of whose membership must consist of representatives from the local business community. This was done in an effort to make job training less the task of government professionals and more the responsibility of people who know firsthand the communities they are serving.

Community policing. Federal, state, and local programs have been experimenting during the 1990s with strategies for involving neighborhood residents in public safety decision-making. As a result, community policing strategies have prompted police officers to get out of their squad cars and into neighborhood association meetings, and they have prompted residents to break down the "us-them" wall that often exists between them and police in distressed urban neighborhoods. Face-to-face interaction between officers and residents becomes a norm, and public safety strategy is built on neighborhood relationships rather than planning sessions in distant, closed administrative buildings.

Faith-based initiatives. Local faith-based organizations have long provided an underappreciated amount of socially beneficial services. As welfare policies have grown more devolutionary in nature, communities have come to more directly rely on these community healers to renew neighborhoods. Their small scale nature, long a main reason why the general public overlooked them, has now become their predominant virtue. President Bush announced the creation of the White House Office of Faith-Based and Community Initiatives in early 2001 precisely in order to shine a light on and assist these small-scale agents.

New urbanism. A band of developers, architects, and city planners have joined together to promote walkable, mixed-use, human-scale communities and neighborhoods. While they are not concerned first and foremost with policy, these new urbanists, as they are called, are frequently engaged in a battle with restrictive zoning ordinances and policies that prevent human-scale design. Beyond this, however, their influence has reached into federal housing policy. New urbanist ideas were central to the U.S. Department of Housing and Urban Development's HOPE VI program, which demolishes high-density, characterless public housing projects, which have become the all-too-familiar symbols of urban despair, and replaces them with mixed-income units built more closely to a traditional neighborhood design.

Community development. Since their appearance more than thirty years ago, community development corporations have sprung up all across America and now number more than 4,000. These nonprofit organizations, dedicated to a relatively small and fixed geographical area and led by people familiar with the community, create affordable housing in low-income areas, rehabilitate old housing stock, and at times, help provide needed social services. They and other community builders have restored confidence among policymakers that neighborhood problems can be effectively confronted by leaders in the neighborhood, without unnecessary layers of bureaucracy burdening them from above. Policymakers in Washington have followed their grassroots lead. Empowerment zone legislation, which targets a range of community renewal initiatives in a fixed geographic area, has increasingly encouraged a more active role for neighborhood residents. And recently, New Market Tax Credits were created through the Community Renewal Tax Relief Act of 2000 to encourage investment in community development organizations whose boards must, by law, have seats occupied by neighborhood residents.

Each of the foregoing is rooted in the idea that federal programs need to be created on—or retrofitted to—the human scale. Each of them represents a loss of confidence that real lives and real communities can be improved by experts in Washington, or even in a statehouse. Each is a confession that programs must be designed to inhabit the community they serve, so to speak, by taking on the face and character of the community. The six foregoing examples are only a sampling. The list could surely be expanded to include instances of educational and housing programs that are trying to "scale down" to the community level. For example, in an effort to restore something of a human scale to schools, the U.S. Department of Education has allotted more than $100 million for large schools across the United States to create smaller learning communities and units within their organizations.

Indeed, as many people have argued in recent years that we need to "scale up" the work of community-based organizations to address large social problems, Washington has recently been engaged "scaling down" its programs to make them fit for neighborhoods. Less attention has been given in recent years to "scaling back" federal social programs by conservatives because of the stark recognition that Washington must be fair to communities and allow them a chance to adapt federal policies to the needs of their blocks, their neighbors, their streets, and their homes.

The Heart of Human Scale

Most of the foregoing policy examples have to do with making programs work both on a small scale and in a holistic way. This trend in federal policy, admittedly, was borne not out of a renewed interest among legislators in the moral value of communities but out of a concern with government efficiency and effectiveness. Policymakers wanted to get the management of publicly funded programs as close to the people served by those programs as possible. The trend was also borne out of a concern with fairness—that is, by a recognition that federal policies in the past too frequently disregarded the concerns of the very people they were ostensibly designed to help.

There is, however, a poignant moral dimension to these policies that we should not overlook. A common thread running through all of them is the acknowledgment, often implicit, that life (and not just government) is simply better when citizens have a say in shaping the forces affecting their communities. And citizens are especially equipped with the habits, skills, and knowledge to manage these forces when joined together in association. For this reason, many (though not all) human-scale policies look to, and even rely upon, the contribution of the little platoons of democracy such as voluntary associations, congregations, local municipalities, and neighborhood associations.

What is so special about so-called "little platoons"? Edmund Burke, who coined the term more than two hundred years ago, explained it best when he wrote that our affection for the "little platoon we belong to in society, is the first principle (the germ as it were) of public affections. It is the first link in the series by which we proceed toward a love to our country and to mankind."[22] In the little platoon we learn the habits of democracy that eventually make it possible for us to love our country.

This understanding of the importance of association has weathered the test of time. Plato wrote 2,500 years ago that there "is indeed no such boon for a society as this familiar knowledge of citizen by citizen. For where men have no light on each other's characters, but are in the dark on the subject, no one will ever reach the rank or office he deserves, or get the justice which is his proper due."[23]

When people are in fellowship with one another, it becomes difficult to be an unrecognized hypocrite. It is hard to hide unfair actions and prejudices. Character becomes as much a part of our estimation of others as their job title. Democracy depends much more upon each citizen's character than upon the secondary characteristics such as titles, power, and money.

That recent human-scale policies have the small platoon as their common denominator is telling. These small platoons, in particular, are nonprofit community-redeeming organizations—congregations, neighborhood associations, community centers, and local chapters of national organizations such as the YMCA and the Salvation Army. The hope policymakers place in these organizations is rooted in the contention that the personal nature of their services will allow for the holism and moral suasion needed to serve people in the best way available.

Treating people holistically means that a service respects their complex set of needs, concerns, and aspirations as a unity. Providing moral suasion means having the authority to influence the habits and choices of a person in a way that the person fully respects. Holism and moral suasion are, in essence, the two key elements that a human scale environment provides. Impersonal environments cannot supply them well. They are the heart of human scale. The most important of all human-scale environments, the family, provides for a full range of needs, and it supplies, for better or worse, the moral habits and beliefs that shape us for life.

As it turns out, neither government nor the market can treat us holistically or with the moral suasion needed for good citizenship. This is the job of civil society—especially in its local manifestations. Local civil society is the chief discovery of federal domestic policy in the late twentieth century. Legislators have learned that they need to fight poverty not with a new policy-panacea but with an army of compassionate people who do not regard "the poor" as a faceless class but as fellow citizens.

Opportunities for Action

What does this mean for future action? There are three opportunities (and surely there are more) that we have inherited from the trend toward human-scale policy which hold great promise for the future.

First, human-scale policies have revealed the importance of organizing our problem-solving efforts around geography more than around issues themselves. When citizens come together to address the needs of a particular neighborhood or region, they must bring together various groups and organizations that have a stake in the area's well-being. This is different from joining a coalition to take on an issue such as homelessness or juvenile crime or run-down schools or race relations. These things are all important, and organizing around issues will always be important and necessary.

Caring for a place, however, is something that brings people together who may vote for different candidates and share divergent opinions on how to address a particular issue. Fixing our sidewalks, helping our students at our school around the corner, keeping our streets safe, helping our community—these are things less prone to ideological manipulation than an issue is. Milwaukee's success in implementing a school voucher system is owing to the ability of groups who usually disagree politically on issues, such as urban African Americans and conservative whites, to come together in common concern for their city's schools. It is much harder to get liberal African Americans and conservative whites to come together at a state or national level to agree on school reform. Without the common concern of place, the issue remains just that—an issue.

Stephen Goldsmith, former mayor of Indianapolis, devolved funds and decision-making authority to the neighborhood level by requiring neighborhoods to create umbrella organizations through which the activity of other associations could be coordinated. Rather than launching issue-specific initiatives, Goldsmith's strategy was neighborhood-specific. The umbrella organizations required various nonprofit and community-serving associations to work together to devise solutions to problems that they shared as a community.

The future of solutions to social problems may very well depend on the degree to which citizens are successful in their geographic orientation. It is easier to motivate people to help find employment for an ex-offender returning to their community from prison than to get them to serve on an "ex-offender task force." A sense of place and obligation to a community helps depoliticize issues and convert them into an everyday concern.

On this front, there exists great opportunity for suburban churches, for instance, to partner with urban congregations by taking up the burden that the latter face in their particular communities. Most large cities have "mega-churches" out in their suburbs, populated by relatively affluent, largely white congregants, who generally have no idea how to design an urban ministry program. Those that have figured it out have generally found that they must come alongside a particular urban congregation, or group of congregations, to help them address a particular set of needs. Those that fail have generally designed an "urban outreach" program that tries to get urban congregations to adapt themselves to the suburban church's idea of a helpful program—whether it is Saturdays spent painting churches or running youth day camps or whatever. Those that figure it out come to understand the unique nature of urban poverty and take on a set of concrete problems as their own, while those who fail force an abstract—even ideological—view of poverty on city dwellers and then scratch their heads in bewilderment when urban pastors do not return their calls.

The second area of opportunity is the use and creation of intermediary organizations. Intermediaries are not a distinct, uniform group. They may be an urban social services agency, a leadership foundation, a large church, a local United Way agency, a community foundation. What intermediaries have in common is the unique ability to build bridges between small, grassroots organizations and larger institutions such as government or foundations. Intermediaries help connect civil society's institutions with the institutions of other sectors.

Intermediaries usually speak the language of the street and the language of the conference room. They help a grassroots urban organization understand how to apply for government funding and manage the funding when it arrives. They also help the bureaucrat understand the dynamic, informal character of the inner-city church that happens to be running a successful but haphazardly managed affordable housing program.

The Good Samaritan in Ottawa County, Michigan, became nationally known when it helped its county become the first in the nation to reduce its welfare caseload to zero after the passage of the federal welfare reform act.[24] It took a contract with the county human services agency and rallied churches together to provide mentoring and individualized attention for former welfare recipients. The Boston United Way brings together grassroots faith-based organizations under its Faith in Action program and helps equip them to more effectively serve their neighborhoods. As an intermediary between local congregations and private funders and other large community-serving agencies, the United Way helps the "little guy" expand the reach and depth of its services.

Intermediaries are especially important in today's world of devolution and faith-based and community initiatives. The trend toward devolving resources to local levels has forced upon states and localities the need to figure out how to produce results, which has in turn forced them to look down to sub-local entities represented by community-based organizations and congregations. How do we take resources and program guidelines originating at a national level and adapt them to the contours of a local community? Local public officials know that they need to root their services strongly at the community level, but they often lack relationships with grassroots leaders. Intermediary organizations can help them solve this dilemma.

Philanthropists, too, who seek to improve a particular community often fund a group of direct service providers without considering how sponsorship of an intermediary organization might help them bring coherence and added efficiency to their giving. Intermediaries are too often overlooked by philanthropists who prefer to fund frontline organizations whose work generates more exciting photos and anecdotes for foundations' annual reports.

The third major opportunity concerns the art of multisector cooperation—or the ability of our market, government, and nonprofit sector organizations to work together for the good of our communities. In a large scale, fragmented society, these three main sectors often operate separately from one another or cooperate only when they have to. At the local level, when they work together, they help overcome this fragmentation and recreate some semblance of community.

At the national level an issue such as "poverty" is generally a problem for government to fix with a variety of programs. The "market" is frequently used to refer to the activity on the New York Stock Exchange where corporate "value" is conceived primarily in terms of stock valuation. At the local level poverty is more than an abstraction or an issue for government to tackle alone, and the market, which has as much to do with work opportunity as anything, is connected to the larger community in a number of ways. Businesses relocate to greener pastures as the neighborhoods around them become unsafe and provide disincentives for recruitment because of poor schools. The local government responds by raising taxes to make up for lost revenue, followed by additional business exoduses. Human services providers fight tremendous difficulties with ultra-tight budgets.

On the other side of the coin, a number of industry sectors such as construction and services such as hotels and branch banking that employ large numbers of entry-level individuals suffer from labor shortages not for a lack people looking for work but because the victims of poverty are largely unprepared for work. Poverty advocates complain that businesses disenfranchise the poor, and businesses complain that social services are inept at preparing people for the real world. They both realize that their worlds are highly interdependent, even if negatively so.

In short, at the local level the concerns and activities of different sectors affect each other all the time. Unfortunately, in their effort to fix problems, many local communities rely on programs and strategies in a way that mirrors the overly sectored national scene. But this is changing. Many communities—and, especially, those under the leadership of an innovative stock of mayors across America in the 1990s—have begun seeing local problems for what they are: the whole community's problem.

Successful local leaders articulate the benefits each sector can expect to reap from investing themselves in cooperation. Businesses that see the problems of poverty affecting their ability to create value for both customers and employees will have an interest in cooperation. Human services are always looking for ways to enhance the employability of their clients, extend access to capital to more low-income families, and create more home ownership among the poor—all areas with which businesses can help.

As communities begin to see the interdependence of economic development, workforce preparedness, public safety, and education, they begin to strategize in multisector ways. The different sectors—market, government, nonprofit—become interested in each other's concerns in a manner difficult to replicate at the national level. National interest groups and corporations can focus on the issue that makes them tick—whether it is fighting child poverty or manufacturing cell phones. Local communities cannot tick at all if they allow their sectors to live in isolation from one another.

Buncombe County, North Carolina, provided access to quality health care to all of its 15,000 uninsured residents not by waiting upon a national solution, but by forming an effective, multisector partnership. The Buncombe County Medical Society in Asheville coordinates an integrated network of physician volunteers, neighborhood clinics, hospitals, and pharmacies. The network leverages the best of what each partner has to offer while serving each one's interests. The network, fueled primarily by physician volunteers who agree to see a set number of uninsured patients per month at no charge, has significantly driven down the cost of hospital charity care and reduced emergency room visits by 50 percent. It has also reduced the costs of expensive treatments by catching health problems sooner and has freed up the county health department to see 50 percent more patients than in the past.[25] On top of this, the partnership has created a unified system of health care out of formerly disparate, disconnected parts. It has created a community of health care where there formerly was none.

Examples like this can be found in welfare-to-work initiatives, public safety programs, mentoring efforts, and more. The key to each is the way in which each partner begins to calculate the community's interest into its own interest. Each partner grows interested in what the other partners have to offer. Each, in sum, begins to see itself as part of a larger good: the community to which it owes its cooperation in exchange for the help, reduced hassle, and added benefit it receives.

By placing attention on geography instead of issues alone, intermediaries instead of frontline providers alone, and multisector cooperation instead of each sector alone, innovators across our societal spectrum can help recreate a human scale wherever it is beneficial to do so. Each of us benefits from the community around us in ways often invisible to us, and each of us has something to give in return even if we are not doing so now. Human-scale environments enable us to recognize these potentialities more easily, and our brightest innovators help us turn them into realities.

For the Good of All

The small platoons of a healthy democracy help bring the large concerns of public life down to the neighborhood level. This, it bears mentioning, is good for all of us—not just for people living in low-income and distressed communities. The culture of BIG pervades every corner of contemporary society. What is important about the three opportunities for action just presented is that each represents an opportunity for affluent mainstream Americans to engage in the life of their larger communities.

When geography rather than an "issue" is the focus of a socially redeeming project; when intermediaries help raise the concerns of the street to conference rooms of statehouses and office buildings; when the barriers between the sectors come down and businesses, governments, and social sector organizations begin to cooperate—then the odds increase that a community's more affluent and mainstream members will see the connection between them and the rest of the community. These opportunities for action help build "bridging capital," which connects the concerns and aspirations of groups that otherwise would not interact.[26] This activity is good not merely because of the benefits that accrue to low-income communities as a result but because of good habits that get cultivated along the way in the lives of all involved.

The underlying theme of this book is that civil society organizations are good not simply for the beneficiaries of their services and activities but for those engaged in them: their managers, their volunteers, their funders. So much attention has been placed in recent years on the functional value of civil society for delivering services to low-income communities. Not as much attention has been placed on the importance of civil society for maturing our moral sensibilities.

Families and schools are expected to incubate habits such as restraint, self-sacrifice, hard work, cooperation, and sound thinking. Voluntary associations, neighborhood organizations, and faith-based groups likewise cultivate the kinds of habits that make democracy work. Together, these small platoons mean a lot for America.

They are the primary means by which the minds and hearts of their members extend beyond themselves to the public, the community, the common good. They are our primary defense against the downward inertial drag that individualism has on our culture, our homes, and our most important institutions. There is little the market or government or large national nonprofit interest groups can do to help turn our self-directed eyes to the community around us. Human-scale society, on the other hand, can make the community part of our natural purview.

Notes

1. Gordon Craig, *Europe Since 1815*, 2nd ed. (New York: Holt, Rinehart and Winston, 1961), 264-65.

2. Christopher Schmitz, *The Growth of Big Business in the United States and Western Europe, 1850-1939* (Cambridge: Cambridge University Press, 1995), 10 ff.

3. R. Shep Melnick, "An American Dilemma," *Wilson Quarterly*, vol. 23, no. 4 (September 1999).

4. See Andres Duany, Elizabeth Plater-Zyberk, and Jeff Speck, *Suburban Nation: The Rise of Sprawl and the Decline of the American Dream* (New York: North Point, 2000), 10-11.

5. Edward Blakely and Mary Gail Snyder, *Fortress America: Gated Communities in the United States* (Washington, D.C.: Brookings, 1997), 7-8.

6. Putnam points out that unlike the fairly recent past, when national membership associations in America were headquartered in diverse cities and towns and had strong local chapter-based activity, today's largest and most powerful membership organizations are headquartered within about ten blocks of one another in Washington, D.C. (*Bowling Alone: The Collapse and Revival of American Community* (New York: Simon and Schuster, 2000), 50-51.

7. Aristotle, *Politics*, 1253a27.

8. Amitai Etzioni, ed., *Rights and the Common Good: The Communitarian Perspective* (New York: St. Martin's, 1995), 22.

9. Putnam's research shows that while volunteering is up, involvement in community projects is down, suggesting that Americans are volunteering more on an individual basis in a program of an organization of which they are a part, such as a church (*Bowling Alone*, 130). He also supplies substantial evidence that along with trust, basic social connections are on the decline, evidenced by declining hospitality, time with neighbors, and so on.

10. *Employer Firms, Establishments, Annual Payroll, and Receipts by Firm Size, 1988-1998*, U.S. Small Business Administration.

11. Tim Petersen, "An Era of Consolidations: Mergers and Acquisitions in the 90s," *Michigan Banker* vol. 11, no. 6 (June 1, 1999): 90 ff.

12. *Historical Tables of the Budget of the United States for Fiscal Year 2002*, U. S. Office of Management and Budget (Washington, DC: Government Printing Office, 2001).

13. *Historical Tables of the Budget*, and the *Statistical Abstract of the United States 2000*, U.S. Census Bureau.

14. Robert Nisbet, *The Quest for Community* (New York: Oxford University Press, 1953), and Kirkpatrick Sale, *Human Scale* (New York: Coward, McCann & Geoghegan, 1980).

15. Peter Berger and Richard John Neuhaus, *To Empower People: The Role of Mediating Structures in Public Policy* (Washington, D.C.: American Enterprise Institute Press, 1977, 1996).

16. Lewis Mumford, *The City in History* (New York: MIF Books, 1961), 331. Mumford cites an early New England practice of forbidding residents from living far enough from the commons that they would forsake their civic obligations during the winter when the weather served as a disincentive to showing up at town meetings.

17. Jane Jacobs, *The Death and Life of Great American Cities* (New York: Random House, 1961), 131-32.

18. See D. T. Williams, "The Dimensions of Education: Recent Research on School Size," *Working Paper Series*, Clemson University, Strom Thurmond Institute of Government and Public Affairs (December 1990), and W. J. Fowler and H. J. Walberg, "School Size, Characteristics, and Outcomes," *Educational Evaluation and Policy Analysis* vol. 13, no. 2 (Summer 1991): 189-202.

19. Curt Coffman and Jim Harter, "A Hard Look at Soft Numbers," *Linking Attitudes to Outcomes* (Lincoln: Gallup Organization, 1999), 1-5.

20. Francis Fukuyama, "Trust: The Social Virtues and the Creation of Prosperity," in *The Essential Civil Society Reader: The Classic Essays*, ed. Don E. Eberly (Lanham, Md.: Rowman & Littlefield, 2000), 262.

21. Putnam, *Bowling Alone*, and *Making Democracy Work: Civic Traditions in Modern Italy* (Princeton: Princeton University Press, 1993).

22. Edmund Burke, *Reflections on the Revolution in France*, ed. J. C. D. Clark (Stanford: Stanford University Press, 2000), 202.

23. Plato, *Laws*, trans. A.E. Taylor, in *The Collected Dialogues of Plato*, eds. Edith Hamilton and Huntington Cairns (Princeton: Princeton University Press, 1961), 738 d-e.

24. For a case study on this organization, see Chapter Three in my *Transforming Charity: Toward a Results-Oriented Social Sector* (Indianapolis: Hudson, 2001).

25. See Dennis Andrulis and Michael Gusmano, *Community Initiatives for the Uninsured: How Far Can Innovative Partnerships Take Us?*, New York Academy of Medicine: Division of Health and Science Policy (August 2000): sec. 2, 29-37.

26. Putnam, *Bowling Alone*, 22-23.

Chapter Three

Individuals and a Healthy Civic Order

Don Eberly

Several years ago, I was called upon to testify before the full Judiciary Committee in the U.S. House of Representatives on the role of popular mass culture in producing the kind of youth alienation and school violence we have witnessed in places like Littleton, Colorado.

I was prepared to talk about how the chief job of every society is to produce a large number of adults who have well-developed consciences, empathy for others, and a willingness to embrace the norms of civilized society. My intention was to illustrate how that process of socialization—led by parents, moral exemplars, and authority figures in the community—should work.

I was prepared to wax on about how, because of technological change, socialization of the young has shifted steadily away from traditional authority—parental, educational, and religious—toward the popular mass culture. It is the culture, I planned to argue, that has become our moral tutor, shaping the values, attitudes, and behaviors of our citizens and increasingly charting the direction of our nation. It is the culture that is the most powerful engine driving social breakdown. And so on.

I was especially hoping to show how the erosion of legitimate social authority at least partially explains why the boundaries of conduct and belief, so grossly exceeded in the case of Littleton's Eric Harris and his hateful ideologies, are now so hard to maintain.

The analysis was not needed. Preceding me in the hearings was a panel of students, led by an articulate twelfth-grader from a large suburban high school, whose function at the hearing was simply to describe her school. What distinguished her high school, she said, was that "no one was in charge." Not the teachers, not the parents, not even the security guards. She added that in the midst of this chaos the school kept adding more and more rules, even though the rules which did exist were never enforced.

Knowing that a picture such as this was worth a thousand words, I dispensed with my statement and merely urged the thirty-five-plus representatives to reflect long and hard on the vivid portrayal they had just witnessed of institutions with their most basic authority hollowed out. Here, in this one public high school, was a microcosm of the entire society.

Welcome to the Republic of the Autonomous Self, where the individual is the sovereign, where "mediating" structures have been leveled, and where rules proliferate and yet lack legitimacy. Those who point to legitimate social authority as an essential ingredient in a well-ordered society often have the charge of nostalgia leveled against them. But the rise of what Robert Bellah called a "radically unencumbered and improvisational self" produces ugly tensions, discord, and national disharmony.

Progressive or Regressive?

What is ironic about contemporary individualism is that it got a tremendous boost from early twentieth-century progressivism, which was aimed at greater national unity and community. For progressives, localized forms of social authority and civic networks conjured up images of corrupt inefficiency presided over by unenlightened nonprofessionals harboring retrograde social attitudes. Bill Schambra, an important voice in today's civil society debates, says that progressives disdained what they viewed as a vast "chaotic jumble of divergent civic institutions and local loyalties" which the state would properly proceed "ruthlessly to extirpate or absorb." The progressive goal was to organize a cadre of qualified professionals trained in the most advanced theories at elite policy schools to replace local officials, who were consistently disparaged as ignorant and untrained. The trouble with this, however, was that centralized expert-driven programs could not help but to materialize into programs governed less by human judgment and more by myriad rules and laws.

However grand the intent of these progressive visionaries might have been and however justified their concerns about the inadequacies of local programs, the progressive movement, critics argue, gave birth to the "governmental assumption" which became the "ubiquitous unchallenged *modus operandi* of the twentieth century." Under this assumption, only national solutions were adequate to confront local problems. Federal government activism became seen as the social panacea. Federal programs would end poverty; Congress would eliminate gangs through new programs; a federal bureau with a well-funded staff of professionals would revitalize any schools that fell into mediocrity. Guided by these operative beliefs, "enlightened" managers assumed the role of trustees over the provision of social services, badly weakening the old civic order with its private, voluntary, and decentralized approach to collective action.

Moreover, the destruction of communities transformed America's traditional sense of individualism (once held in check by a Protestant respect for the public good) to one embracing an ideal of absolute autonomy for the individual. Today's individualism presents the self as the only sovereign: autonomous, empowered, and dangerously detached from transcendent morality or social restraints. It has turned many spheres of human activity into a battleground for personal advancement at the expense of cooperative behavior.

Radical Autonomy

The results of this radically emancipated self are anything but progressive or pleasant. Rather, a self freed of meaningful social obligation is a weak self, standing alone with his or her desires and fleeting amusements at hand—and little else. A viable civic order requires more than that. It requires selves who see their own well-being as part of a larger social order and are thus willing to act on behalf of the wider community. The commonplace view that individuals are stronger and healthier the more they are freed from legitimate forms of social authority disregards the costs we bear by raising generations of children who do not believe they owe anything to anyone. Wayward atoms rushing past one another but never joining together in service of a common purpose is hardly a picture of national greatness but of weakness. Like entropy, it is a picture of an unraveling entity that has seen better days.

One consequence of radical autonomy is that we are transformed from "one nation, indivisible" to a balkanized place characterized by what historian Arthur Schlesinger aptly described as "the fragmentation, resegregation, and tribalization of American life." A related result is that people become more self-centered. Social analyst and pollster Daniel Yankelovich has spent his entire adult life studying the shifting sands of American moral attitudes, and concluded that the vast changes in our society can be explained by one underlying seismic shift. We have moved, he said, from a sense of "duty to others" to a "duty to self."

Collapsing under the weight of radical autonomy is any workable notion of the common good. Yankelovich's observation tracks with what I found in doing extensive research on citizen attitudes for a book on the state of American civil society. In surveying the description of society by citizens themselves, I repeatedly found them using words like fraying, fracturing, and fragmenting to describe the world around them. Citizens were saying essentially that too many people are out for themselves. "What chills me about the future," wrote one, "is a general sense of the transformation of our society from one that strengthens the bonds between people to one that is, at best, indifferent to them." There is "a sense of an inevitable fraying of the net of connections between people at many critical intersections, of which the marital knot is only one. Each fraying accelerates another. A break in one connection, such as attachment between parents and children, puts pressure on other connections such as marriage." With enough fraying, "individuals lose that sense of membership in the larger community which grows best when it is grounded in membership in the small one."

Fraying communities, fractured families, a fragmenting nation—journalists, scholars, and citizens alike seem to agree that American society, in too many ways, has been pulling apart.

Democracy under Strain

The result has been an increasingly self-centered, litigious, and arbitrary society. The social space where decisions are made on the basis of self-interest, competition, and the struggle for power expands, while the space that is truly voluntary and consensual, where people of goodwill and civilized values can join together in rational deliberation, shrinks. The handshake gives way to the omnipresence of the law. The law, in turn, becomes overworked and arbitrary. Society feels like an engine running low on oil—things heat up. This is alarming because, as Mary Ann Glendon of Harvard University has put it, "If history teaches us anything, it is that democracy cannot be taken for granted. There are *social and cultural* conditions that are more or less favorable to its success."

Democracy requires a capacity for trust and collaboration, at least on the small scale of face-to-face community. America's founders talked about the ingredients of civic virtue, such things as sentiments, affections, manners, and duty to the common good. These core qualities are the first link in a long series of steps whereby, as Burke put it, "we develop our love for mankind" generally. In other words, the outer order of society is directly linked to the inner order of our souls.

Most democratic reforms today, however, are directed toward fixing the procedural aspects of the state without addressing the underlying cultural and social crisis. As the state has expanded and individual restraint waned, public life has been reduced to what Michael Sandel calls "proceduralism," leaving the public realm little purpose except to maximize private opportunity. The problems of money, declining participation, and the uneven distribution of power are indeed serious problems, but democracy is fragile in a way that no campaign finance reform and no amount of increased voter participation can cure. The more serious problems of American democracy have to do with the erosion of democratic character and habit. A society in which men and women are morally adrift and intent chiefly on gratifying their appetites will be a disordered society no matter how many people vote. We must recover the democratic citizen through restored communities, functioning social institutions, and a renewed culture.

Proceduralism places an impossible burden on the state. In a well-ordered society, the state is subordinate to other sectors of society and is thought ill-suited to carry the full load of mediating every dispute. In the good society, politics is peripheral, not the central means for advancing individual happiness.

The state consumes, but does little to resupply, the social glue generated by voluntary cooperative endeavor, the trademark of civil society. In fact, the state frequently hinders and displaces efforts toward this voluntary cooperation, resulting in a vicious cycle of state expansion and societal enervation. As Bill Schambra observes, "[W]hen government moves aggressively into the civic realm to take up the slack where mediating structures may be faltering, their authority is thereby only further undermined."

When the law is forced to compensate for the absence of social restraint and manners, it becomes the catalyst for a rights-based individualism and degenerates into an arbitrary tool of the politically organized. When only the law and politics arbitrate human affairs, even the most basic and intimate human relations become political, and the spirit of consensual problem-solving is replaced by the raw assertion of power. Life in democratic society thus becomes a zero-sum struggle of all against all. A right conferred upon one group becomes an obligation imposed on another. The pursuit of the good and just society is reduced to a dehumanizing struggle over rules. Democracy's "habits of the heart" degenerate into cold proceduralism, and its institutions become exhausted from overload.

If politics is to recover its civic voice, Sandel says, "it must once more ask questions society has forgotten how to ask," questions about ends beyond rational self-interest and economic and political advantage-seeking. To thrive, democracy needs the help of nongovernmental sectors, including strong social institutions and a healthy culture. Without them, a culture of excess prevails and awakens an appetite for things that no viable democracy can offer—the simultaneous expansion of the law and a widening search for freedom from the abuses of the law. The law is forced to enter where gentler forms of governance such as manners and social norms retreat, ultimately eroding human dignity and freedom.

This restless search for human progress through legal reforms creates a politicized society and a state that expands radically even as its competence and legitimacy ebb. The law degenerates into an arbitrary tool of the politically organized. A right conferred upon one group becomes an obligation imposed on another. One person's gain is another's loss. The legal system is forced to find ever-finer balances and boundaries between conflicting parties and claims. People expect the law simultaneously to confer the right of sexual freedom as well as freedom from sexual assault; to guarantee gender and racial advantages for some and the protection against reverse discrimination for others; to protect the rights of criminal offenders and the rights of their victims; to guard the rights of free speech while initiating new rights against the insult of hateful speech; to defend the rights of both individuals and communities; and so on.

Never before has the law been called upon to split conflicting demands with such exasperating precision. The justice system begins to resemble a harried referee who has the impossible task of policing a sport that is both choked by rules and overwhelmed by infractions. The pursuit of a just society is reduced to a perpetual fight over what the rules should be.

Disordered Liberty, Crippled Authority

When only the law and politics arbitrate human affairs, everything becomes politicized—even the most basic and private forms of human association and action, such as one's sexual practices. The private, sacred, and mystical aspects of life become the basis for social and political agitation.

Analysts such as Jean Elshtain, author of *Democracy on Trial,* identify several troubling consequences of the rise of the private self and collapse of the public good. When civic space declines, a politics of displacement emerges to fill the gap. This "complete collapse of a distinction between public and private [is] anathema to democratic thinking," says Elshtain. It follows two trajectories.

> In the first, everything private—from one's sexual practice to blaming one's parents for one's lack of self-esteem—becomes grist for the public mill. In the second, everything public—from the grounds on which politicians are judged, to health politics, to gun regulations—is privatized and played out in a psychodrama on a grand scale.

The public arena becomes a place where, in Elshtain's words, "[I] and my fleeting angers, resentments, sentiments, and impulses," unmediated by local institutions, become important public business. Not only is society politicized, the "personal is political." Nothing personal remains exempt from "political definition, direction, and manipulation."

What we see about us is the steady replacement of an ordered liberty with the libertarianism of John Stuart Mill, in which freedom is absolute, the self is unbounded by even private morality and convention, and one's actions are protected even from social disapproval. Whereas liberty was once conceived of as having properties beyond the self, bound by morality and religion and tied to the interests of the commonwealth, today "the individual is the sole repository and arbiter of all values," as historian Gertrude Himmelfarb put it, and is thus in "an adversarial relationship to society and the state." This is a liberty, says Himmelfarb, which "is a grave peril to liberalism itself."

Many of the most corrupting viruses are now being borne along not by sinister politicians but by an entertainment and information media culture whose omnipresence is displacing the core social institutions that once shaped and molded the democratic citizen. Whereas parents, priests, and pedagogues once presided over the socialization of the young, now television, film, music, cyberspace, and the celebrity culture of sports and entertainment dominate this process of shaping youthful attitudes and beliefs. It is popular mass culture that largely informs our most basic understanding of society, our public life, our obligations to each other, and even the nature of the American experiment.

The function of culture in a free society is to establish and maintain boundaries around beliefs and behaviors considered necessary for maintaining a democratic society. The culture both reflects and influences what people think is right and proper. American culture has usually stressed moral rectitude but has always permitted wide latitude for abnormal beliefs and behavior to operate freely at the margins of society, as long as it stayed there. We had "red light districts," for example, which one was free to frequent, albeit at the risk of exposure and public shame. But even these mild social constraints crumble when everybody is electronically hardwired and what is marginal becomes mainstreamed at the flip of a TV remote or the click of a computer mouse.

Much of what passes for culture today is, in fact, anticulture. Its chief aim is to emancipate, not restrain, to give free reign to human appetite, not to moderate it. The role of entertainment, we are frequently told by entertainers themselves, is to challenge and stretch standards. "Break the rules!" "Have no fear!" "Be yourself!" are the common themes within mainstream cultural programming, and they are designed to discredit traditional forms of authority. The trouble, of course, is that no society can long sustain itself if such emancipatory maxims are actually adopted by the larger share of the population.

Which takes us back to the congressional hearings on school violence. Without a healthy culture maintaining the conditions for human flourishing, we evolve steadily into a custodial democracy, mildly authoritarian, in which more and more transactions are supervised by the state. The anarchy of the school is but a passing phase that creates the desire for more laws and restrictions.

This is how social conflict erodes freedom. People are either ruled by character and civility or they are ruled by cops and lawyers. Anarchy produces injury, which produces lawsuits followed by a thickening layer of defensive measures. Not many years ago, parents from small towns would have recoiled in horror to think that electronic surveillance would become commonplace in our schools, much less that uniformed police would one day roam the halls. "These are schools," they would probably have said, "not prisons." Today, by contrast, polls show that most parents now embrace these symbols of a police state, where their children gather, no less.

Such is the course of freedom's erosion. Gone is freedom of the most precious kind: the freedom of parents to send their children to schools where safety and order are maintained through instruction in the gentle virtues of respect and civility, not the chilling presence of weapons detectors and armed police. Gone is the freedom of children to proceed through life unharassed and unhurried, enjoying the innocence of youth as long as it should be theirs to enjoy.

This is the delusion of the modern libertine. When social institutions and authority collapse and the capacity to govern human affairs through voluntary, consensual means erodes, all roads lead to the state—especially the courts and innumerable social agencies forced by default to become the caretakers of fragile families and poorly socialized individuals, from the unruly children of the urban underclass to the spoiled and dysfunctional latchkey kids of our prosperous suburbs. The fragmentation about us, which libertarians of all stripes tend to view benignly, is leading inevitably and ironically to the very statism they claim to oppose.

A society in which atomized and poorly socialized individuals continually organize to use the state against each other is a society in which the individual and the state are advancing but civil society, a place of consensual and voluntary action, is in retreat. It is also a society in which individuals have grown weaker and weaker in the face of more and more powerful, yet impersonal, forms of social authority and enforcement. This individualism, which we labored so tirelessly to secure for ourselves in the previous century, is of a very flimsy variety.

Fighting Atomization with Cultural Reformation

The solution to our weakened state is to recover the individual person in civil society; not the individual captured in identity politics or ethnic tribalism, but tied once again to the intermediary institutions of family and community. This understanding of the citizen—not as tribesman, client, or consumer but as a builder of the commonwealth—can close the gap between the individual and the state. In fact, democracy's survival depends on the presence of just such a democratic disposition, habit, and outlook among the members of society, which must be carefully nourished, generation by generation. Tocqueville captured the loss of common democratic values when he wrote, "Without ideas in common, there is no common action. There may still exist human beings, but not a social entity. In order for society to exist and, even more, to prosper, it is necessary that the spirits of all citizens be held together by certain leading ideas."

The job before us, then, is to revive the spiritual and moral dimensions of democracy. Sandel calls for the replacement of rights-based individualism with the "classical republican tradition" where private interests are "subordinated to the public good and in which community life takes precedence over individual pursuits." The classical republican tradition offers a vision of the individual, not merely in competition with others through the market nor in conflict with others via the state, but in cooperation through civil society. The central concern of civic republicanism as a public philosophy is renewing a substantive and vigorous democracy by expanding the role of the mediating institutions of civil society.

The civil society movement revisits a rich but long-neglected feature of Western moral and political thought. The concept of civil society is rooted largely, though certainly not exclusively, in the Christian natural-law tradition. The emphasis within this tradition, which is to view civil society as a realm independent of the state, was critical to developing a philosophy of limited government and ordered liberty. Government remains limited to the extent that nongovernmental institutions play a vital offsetting role.

If our current public philosophy is impoverished, as many believe, the question becomes: If human beings are made for civil society, and civil society is to be the centerpiece of a new public philosophy, what must be done to revitalize it? How can old civic forms and institutions be replaced with new ones that more directly respond to today's need for connection? How can the excesses of the sensate culture be moderated? How can social and technological change be harnessed to strengthen voluntary human association? And how should this effort be organized?

Public policy certainly plays a role, although a limited one for the reasons noted earlier. Devolution of power to state, local, and community-based institutions can continue to move decision-making authority downward and outward to citizens. Government support and resources can be directed toward "protecting, reinforcing, and nurturing the varied groups" of society, as Robert Nisbet put it.

Just as policy will play a part, so will dynamic new social movements. James Q. Wilson and others have traced various social reform movements that arose in American history to uplift moral standards. These movements had a common desire to instill character by treating the individual as capable of and responsible for exercising self-control. Social ills were confronted by recovering "a self-activating, self-regulating, all-purpose inner control."

The institutions that effectively socialize people are private and local, according to Wilson, which means that Americans should identify, evaluate, and encourage those local, private efforts that seem to do the best job at reducing drug abuse, inducing people to marry, persuading parents, especially fathers, to take responsibility for their children, and exercising informal social controls over neighborhood streets.

These private efforts include the fatherhood movement, the marriage movement, the character movement, the teen-abstinence movement, and many others.

The most urgent work of all may be pursuing moral and cultural reformation. Civil society is, after all, a moral and social order that transcends each person and requires each to yield some cherished personal autonomy in order to restore the legitimacy of community institutions. As Bill Schambra puts it, the problems of society "are above all moral and cultural phenomena" which in a free society necessarily involve "questions of right and wrong personal behavior, of decent and indecent individual behavior, in short, the questions that are so troubling to us today."

Modernity and the public philosophies it has spawned have placed the sovereign, autonomous self at the center of all things, making decisions of right and wrong strictly contingent on human choice. Ethical relativists convinced the nation—for a time—that education, technology, and professional expertise alone could preserve social order and harmony without the aid of morality.

Needless to say, experience has proven this utopian vision deficient, and more and more people know it. The current challenge is not merely one of reforming or reconfiguring the administrative systems of government, nor of revving up the economy or carrying technology and science to new heights. The central challenge for Americans is to build a civil and humane society.

There is much to cheer in current talk about community and civil society, but the difficulty of the challenge makes the outcome highly uncertain. Czech President Vaclav Havel foresees profound change ahead in the new millennium— "a new 'post-modern phase' where everything is possible and almost nothing is certain." Nothing short of a new spiritual vision of global dimensions, says Havel, will save human civilization. To strengthen families, neighborhoods, and civic associations, we will first have to recognize that these institutions are essential to a civil and humane society, and then marshal the courage and moral strength necessary to restore them. The truth is, we must look beyond man—beyond what Havel calls an "arrogant anthropocentrism" that has dogged this century—and find moral wisdom in truths that transcend our existence.

The struggle under way in the United States is literally to revive the lost soul of a nation, to effect a broad-based moral, civic, and democratic renewal. A new moral order centered upon transcendent reality, the basic moral worth of people, and the inherently moral nature of human community must undergird the movement toward civil society.

This work must be inspired by hope. Few people knew more about society's tendencies than Tocqueville himself. He wrote with an awareness of the impending storm that is now upon us, and he predicted the unraveling of communities, the rise of atomized individualism, and our absorption in a culture of "paltry pleasures." Even so, he was an optimist. He believed that Americans were capable of assessing their condition and mustering the resources to confront it. The challenge is for people of intelligence and goodwill to find a common moral language for public life. On this, the future of democracy may rest.

Note

Portions of the present chapter appeared as "What Chills Me About the Future," *American Outlook* (Fall 1999), and "Renewing American Culture," *American Outlook* (Winter 1999). Permission to reproduce these articles in modified form has been generously granted by the Hudson Institute.

PART TWO

Voluntary Associations, Public Policy, and the Marketplace

Chapter Four

Voluntary Associations and the Remoralization of America

Don Eberly

As the nation searches for civic and social renewal, it is important to ask where the public policy debate is today compared to where it was five years ago. Has the role of voluntary associations in producing American social and moral renewal been more widely embraced? In the best of American civic traditions, we must ask how we can effectively organize social action outside of the state, specifically focusing on expanding the role of voluntary associations and privately sponsored social movements as the mechanisms for social renewal.

Historic Reversal

For many decades conventional wisdom assumed that a major reversal of the welfare state was simply not in the cards. Perhaps some trimming was needed here and a minor correction was needed there, but there would be no fundamental reversal in the basic assumptions. The entire weight of sophisticated opinion—buttressed by every prestigious school of public policy in this nation—was that increasing segments of American society would steadily come under the managerial supervision of a credentialed, enlightened, bureaucratic elite.

The fact that we are now instead talking mostly about the miracle-working power of local faith-based charities, which in their ragtag existence represent the antithesis of the public administration state, is nothing short of remarkable. Their very existence, not to mention their effectiveness, is an affront to the pedigreed and professionalized social service bureaucracy. The dominant idea in this country is no longer the progressive view that the problems of community and

of human failings can be effectively confronted by a top-down, rule-driven welfare state.

New Assumptions, Old Habits

Changes in governing assumptions, however, have not been accompanied by
substantial changes in governing realities. While the appetite for government—
at least the voracious kind—has been tamed, there has been little evidence of an
appetite for significantly reforming it.

On the liberal side, ideological objectives have been adjusted somewhat. Liberals no longer reflexively think of "big government" answers and are more attuned to the issue of government costs and limits. There is a wider acceptance of
the market among liberals, and a greater likelihood to promote social goals
through tax credits rather than new entitlements.

Liberals know that they need to be for more than government, but they are
not entirely sure what that might be. Gone is the pretense that government has
all the answers, but government is still the most significant, if not the only, force
in society.

Though lip service is paid by some to civil society, there are few mechanisms
other than the government that vie for legitimacy among liberals. In the vast
majority of cases, liberals still see the apparatus of the state—government agencies, regulations, and income transfers—as the solution of first resort, not last
resort.

Conservatives have continued to rhetorically advance their political ideal of
government downsizing, although they clearly have come up against the limits
of limited government. There is dramatically less ardor behind the proposition
that "government *is* the problem." Ideological attacks on big government have
failed, and even backfired, for lack of moral and practical imagination. They
have recognized that they cannot achieve a number of objectives without a
strong, albeit limited, government, but they lack a compelling public philosophy
to orient their action.

For all of the talk in recent years of new politics and new paradigms, neither
liberal nor conservative positions represent a significant point of departure. The
debate appears deadlocked on the issue of government—how much, how little—
but all within a fairly narrow range of disagreement, and hence the perception
among ideological constituencies that the parties are now mirror images of each
other.

Compassionate Conservatism

Enter compassionate conservatism. Compassionate conservatism represents a
possible way out of the conundrum: it represents neither government activism
nor passivity. It presents a vision for increased public, though not for the most

part governmental, action. It triangulates the ideological claims of big-government liberalism and a pure laissez-faire conservatism. It takes the mantle of compassion, long monopolized by liberals, while adding a practically useful modifier to the noun conservatism.

Most importantly, by its very nature, compassionate conservatism accentuates the failings of government agencies. The very act of spotlighting the successes of local charities, with their paltry budgets and untrained workers, bludgeons the credibility of welfare state liberalism—flush with funds and trained professionals—in a way that fiscal conservatism never could have.

Compassionate conservatism takes the policy debate, as well as conservatism itself, in a new direction—from a negative to a positive proposition, from sterile antistatism to an elevating vision for society. In 1962, Clinton Rossiter, writing in his book *Conservatism,* argued that conservatism could not govern for long on the basis of a sterile antistatism. He said that confusions in conservative thought weakened conservatism's position in the debate and set back "the advance of social justice, the solution of persistent problems of a complex industrial society, and the identification and defense of the primary values in our tradition."

Compassionate conservatism confronts this philosophical void within conservatism. Voluntary associations add an important dimension to public philosophy. A limited government philosophy in the face of social disorder is only part of the equation, and hardly adequate. To maintain, on the one hand, that the social needs of human beings are not solved by government action, must not be seen as suggesting that social problems do not exist or that they will disappear on their own. The challenge, as Richard Cornuelle, author of *Reclaiming the American Dream* states, is to "call upon the imaginative exercise of voluntary altruistic efforts to invigorate a widespread sense of responsibility for social well-being."

And, by so doing, compassionate conservatism speaks proactively to the urgent need of our time. The great challenge of the 1980s and 1990s was to reign in government and revive a moribund economy. The great challenge in the twenty-first century is to rebuild nongovernmental institutions—to not merely replace government with the economic market, but to replace more and more of the public sector with a viable social sector. The challenge before us now is to add an equal commitment to build up the good society to our determination to correct bad government.

Today, the question before us is: how do we create a humane and virtuous society? In the case of humane, the question is: how can we encourage more and more people to take up the burden of becoming "their brother's keeper" in the context of our communities? In regard to virtue, we must ask: how do we create a society in which more and more individuals are regularly induced to choose the path of virtue, and are rewarded for doing so?

President George W. Bush's compassionate conservatism addresses the first question directly. It reflects a vision for a humane society in which we rely more on private, community-based, often faith-oriented charities to confront poverty and social dysfunction. It puts in place a new cornerstone for our social policy: the idea that private, faith-based charities can be more effective in reducing poverty because they are personal, challenging, and spiritual. Compassionate conservatism throws twentieth century welfare policy on its head: it treats the whole person—body, mind, and soul—and treats the person, not in isolation, but in relationship with his fellows in community.

The new thesis, which is that only human persons can meet human needs, is essentially incontestable. Bureaucracy is inherently fragmenting and alienating. Government cannot and should not attempt to deliver love, meaning, and spiritual regeneration. By virtue of their training and employment, bureaucratic "service providers" compartmentalize and treat people as clients and problems to be managed.

Compassionate conservatism offers the framework for a new policy agenda and more. Its popularity signals the possibility of both a new era and new approaches to confronting poverty, which could produce sweeping change in the twenty-first century. This is essential to the meaning of compassionate conservatism. But it means more: it addresses the second part of the equation, which has less to do with the economic poverty of the poor and more to do with the moral poverty of the poor and nonpoor alike.

Compassionate conservatism, as a coherent and compelling public philosophy, points us toward the need to recover virtue throughout the majority of society, apart from which we are left with partial remedies directed selectively to the poor. To encourage virtue and character among the poor while offering implied approval of the irresponsibility of all others through our silence will be justifiably seen by the poor as unfair.

The moral pathologies afflicting American society are no respecters of class, ethnicity, or geographic boundaries. The problems of divorce, cohabitation, fatherlessness, out-of-wedlock pregnancy, abortion, and a host of other moral ills are not confined to the poor, even though the painful consequences of these ills fall disproportionately on them, and especially their children. In fact, many of the very moral ills that we lament among the poor migrated into poor communities from the middle and upper classes, and thus basic fairness suggests that we direct some of our reforming zeal to all Americans, not merely the poor.

Even though we have seen some recent stabilization of our worst social trends, such as violent crime, teen pregnancy, and divorce, many of these social indicators are still very high by historical standards. And, to repeat, they are not confined to the poor, nor will simply targeting the poor reverse them. In fact, what is most remarkable about social deviance today is the extent to which it is practiced in its many forms by persons living above, and often well above, the official poverty level.

Closely linked is the question of how we deal with the continued debasement of our popular mass culture, which affects all classes and which is increasingly the engine driving social breakdown across the income categories.

Values: Public But Not Necessarily Governmental Action

So what do we do about America's values crisis? The American people continue to register stratospheric levels of concern about values and the state of our social institutions, which can be taken as good news. But what cannot be drawn from a more careful look at public opinion is a sweeping mandate for governmental action to restore moral values. The people do not think government can or should do much to promote morality or religion. Somehow, they have lodged deep within their memory bank a recollection of how America confronted moral and spiritual breakdown in the past.

Which leaves us with this profound disconnect. Americans rank moral renewal as the most important public problem and they are longing for public action, but they do not mostly have in mind political action. What is peculiar about all of this is the relative absence in our public debate of any concrete discussion about methods for social change other than elections and lawmaking, even by conservatives for whom voluntary action outside of the state would appear to come naturally.

The story of urban crime, drug and alcohol addictions, promiscuity, and the breakdown of social institutions, is not new in America. What is unique about our past in relationship to these moral conditions is that their existence produced a tremendous flourishing of new voluntary associations aimed at moral and social reform. What is curious about the present is that this same response has not yet taken shape, at least not in similar dramatic form.

There is a strong hint in the pages of history that voluntary associations became the means of social correction when other forms of public action, such as legislative change, fell short. Private associations and moral reform movements have often produced progress after the realization set in that government either could not or would not do these things.

The failure of conservatives to produce more than limited progress on a moral agenda in the Congress may cause growing numbers of Americans to organize for social change outside of the political process, which from a conservative standpoint is mostly where social change belongs. It would be a good thing if citizens overcame their frustration over gridlock in politics by directing their energies toward creating voluntary reform societies in the social sector.

Renewing the nongovernmental sector of civil society first requires recapturing in our political and social imaginations the central role that voluntary associations have historically played in our system. Widespread ignorance of our own history hinders a more fulsome embrace of voluntary associations. It is awareness of this remarkable American legacy of problem-solving through voluntary societies and movements that has itself often nurtured the impulse to social reform.

American history is filled with remarkable success stories of social change being produced by private voluntary initiative, and this heritage of voluntary action offers important insights into how we might promote cultural change again today. Says historian John G. West, "if irreligion and immorality dominated society, it was the responsibility of Christians themselves to form private reform associations to combat these evils—to convert people and to promote virtue."

According to West, religious believers organized "scores of voluntary associations" for evangelism and social reform. They formed groups to confront poverty, of course, by teaching reading and writing to the poor, reforming prisons, and reducing alcohol abuse. But their energetic reform societies also took aim at ills affecting the larger population. West concludes: "This multitude of private associations transformed American society in a way that few government programs could."

Today, we think of voluntary action in fairly constricted terms. We immediately think of organizing aid for the poor through volunteerism and local nonprofits, often invoking Alexis de Tocqueville's famous reference to volunteerism and charitable initiatives for support. But Tocqueville's description of Americans' tendency to create and join voluntary associations is rarely even mentioned as the antidote to wider social breakdown and cultural disintegration.

Tocqueville, Voluntary Associations, and the Limits of Public Policy

Contrary to this limited view of civil society, Tocqueville's description was of a people who thought and acted as though most of the society's work was to be done through voluntary associations. He said: "Americans of all ages, all stations in life, and all types of dispositions are forever forming associations . . . of a thousand different types—religious, moral, serious, futile, very general and very limited, immensely large and very minute. Americans combine to give fetes, found seminaries, build churches, distribute books, and send missionaries to the antipodes. Hospitals, prisons and schools take shape that way."

Finally, he said, "if they want to proclaim a truth or propagate some feeling by the encouragement of a great example, they form an association." In other words, if Americans wanted to advance a moral idea for the betterment of society, they formed a private reform society. If they wanted to raise social standards, they formed a private association. Whatever the concern—social or moral—they formed an association.

This habit of acting independently on behalf of important public business was, according to Tocqueville, America's most unique and remarkable character trait. And it is a trait that is important to fully capture. This was private action by citizens, operating in association with others, to bring about public improvement. It was public action, though not governmental. It was not purely private as in the pursuit of business profit. Nor was it private action organized in every case to effect change in government policy.

There are many problems that will continue to occupy the government, for which the government may be the lead, if not the only, solution: international conflict, terrorism, global environmental challenges, domestic law enforcement, and much more. But the most pressing issues of our time are social and cultural in nature, for which easy government solutions are not available.

Government cannot begin to put the connecting tissue back in society. It is ill equipped to reconstruct traditional moral beliefs within America's cultural institutions. The best policies are incapable of restoring courtship, making fathers responsible for their children, restore shock or shame where it once existed, or recovering legitimate social authority to institutions that have been hollowed out by an ideology of individual autonomy.

It is doubtful that the problem of abortion will be solved predominantly through legislative strategies. Marvin Olasky has written about how concerned citizens reduced high rates of abortion at the turn of the twentieth century through broad-based strategies in the communities of America centering on persuasion and the compassionate care of women caught in crisis pregnancies. In the past, America solved its moral problems through voluntary action aimed at remoralization in the wider society combined with direct aid to individuals caught in crisis.

Although the government can offer bold and decisive action in the face of an economic recession or a military threat, it cannot in the same fashion offer bold action to reverse cultural breakdown. In a disordered society, a heavy reliance on political authority to renew the nonauthoritative sector of culture can quickly become more disease than cure. Law cannot eradicate the vast majority of cultural and moral problems about us.

The Multisector Society

The conservative contribution to the world has been to remind Americans that we are a multisector society; that the state is only one of several equally important sectors; that the state is a subsidiary of society, not its master; and that ideally the state should be much smaller. The problem is that when conservatives address all that is wrong with government, they think mostly in terms of two sectors. One sector, the public sector, is more or less synonymous with the vast domain of government. The counterpart to the public sector is presented as the "private" sector, which is usually synonymous with the market mechanism. When people think of the private sector, they think mostly of free enterprise, or for-profit business activity.

The choice conservatives present is: government versus business, with the suggestion that we have a lot less of the former and more of the latter. The struggle is presented as involving these two sectors exclusively. Each has powerful allies, and each is engaged in a continuous tug-of-war for power, legitimacy, and resources. On the occasions when American politics can be said to be truly polarizing, the conflict almost always has to do with this state-versus-market dichotomy.

Thanks to this government-market dualism, we know much about the state and market mechanism, but we have very little awareness of the role of the nonmarket social sector. This philosophical polarity leaves a vast gaping hole in what was once a more embracing American public philosophy. It leaves under-represented what may be America's most enduring and consequential sector: the voluntary, or independent sector, whose purpose is neither political nor economic, but social improvement.

We have a language for the governmental. Political debate is usually about authorizing a program or approving or disapproving appropriations for an endless list of public agencies bearing arcane acronyms, all based upon analysis from CBO or OMB. We have a language for the economic marketplace: quarterly profit-and-loss statements and analysis of corporate performance. CNN supplies us with hourly financial reports. Professional analysts and ordinary Internet traders watch the stock market.

There is practically no language to describe the social sector, which raises and spends hundreds of billions of dollars, employs millions, and attracts tens of billions of dollars' worth of uncompensated volunteer time. Those who work in it are not even sure what to call it. Some refer to it as the independent sector, calling attention to its independence from the state. Others refer to it as the social sector to highlight its social as opposed to economic function. The more historical term, preferred in academic circles, is civil society.

It must be said that America does not lack a vital nonprofit sector. America has thousands upon thousands of voluntary and civic organizations, many of them quite large and visible in most of our communities. But many of them share the assumptions of public sector bureaucracy. Like the YMCA and YWCA, they started out with a clear-cut religious and moral mission, which has since been largely lost. The challenge in our time is to either reform the old or replace the existing civic structure with that which confronts the moral needs of our time—in other words, to build new voluntary organizations which are committed to remoralization.

One begins to see the outlines emerging today of a new renaissance in private reform movements. Such programs are Best Friends, Elayne Bennett's abstinence program for young girls; the Marriage Savers movement; the responsible fatherhood movement in which I have had a part; and movements too numerous to mention aimed at recovering ethics and character.

The Role of Policy: Identify, Evaluate, Encourage

Where, might we ask, does public policy fit in helping to spur a renaissance in voluntary associations? James Q. Wilson, who has tracked social reforms throughout American history, maintains that the institutions that have imparted character, maintained order, and socialized the young have been private, not public. That being the case, the job of public policy, says Wilson, "is to *identify, evaluate and encourage* those local, private efforts that seem to do the best job at reducing drug abuse, inducing the young to marry, persuading parents, especially fathers, to take responsibility for their children, and exercising informal social controls over neighborhood streets."

So, the highest priority for public officials may be to simply "identify, evaluate and encourage" private initiative. This can take any number of forms, including:

Hold hearings for the purpose of spotlighting successes.

Mandate a new data collection and research agenda for the federal government focusing on social and fiscal health factors associated with moral wellness.

Conduct site visits for the purpose of calling attention to local successes.

Sponsor community forums on cultural issues such as teen pregnancy, youth violence, marriage, and fatherhood.

Help to found public initiatives.

Consider directing more public monies to private groups that are involved in community-based remoralization, such as teen abstinence, alternatives to abortion, or responsible fatherhood projects.

Provide block grant funds to states for the purpose of local charitable tax credits.

Make the federal charitable tax deduction more generous.

Challenge corporations and philanthropic foundations to be more supportive of private initiatives aimed at moral and social reform.

Conclusion

In his book on American conservatism, Clint Rossiter states that conservatism's "indisputable and indispensable achievement" in the past was its skillful "sponsorship and leadership of voluntary associations." This great proclivity for forming associations is the very source of progress, he said, "because it pools the hopes and talents of free individuals and breeds natural leaders; it brings stability because it balances the American ideal of self-reliance against the universal urge for communal association; it defends liberty because it serves as a buffer between man and government, doing things for him that he cannot do for himself and must not let government do for him."

The challenge before us is take seriously the need both to reform bad government and to build a humane and virtuous society, and to do that through the skillful sponsorship of voluntary associations and privately organized initiatives designed to bring about moral renewal.

Chapter Five

Targeting Recovery to Low-Income Families

Don Eberly

Poverty's Challenge to the Civic Sector

The growing signs of civic renewal in America will be celebrated by most and will assuage concerns about whether America is in a state of civic decline, as some have argued. Still, these very trends may raise as many questions as they answer for public policy analysts, especially regarding the extent to which the social sector can adequately address America's most enduring and obdurate problems such as poverty. There is less doubt that America is moving toward a social renaissance than there is skepticism regarding how much that renewal will benefit the most destitute communities in America.

In short, for those who believe that renewal movements must be measured by how they improve life for all Americans, and perhaps especially the poor, euphoria may be premature. One must ask whether the increased social capital taking shape within the middle class—whether in the form of inherited wealth, increased personal involvement, or proliferating nonprofits—will in any meaningful way improve the prospects for the poorest Americans? Can this renewal movement, if it can be called that, be captured on behalf of the neediest Americans?

It would be a mistake to conclude based upon this evidence that all is well— or even significantly on the mend—in every community of America. With exceptional economic growth and near record levels of employment throughout the 1990s, it appears that the national public debate has merely shifted to other subjects. But according to officials of thirty major cities recently surveyed, the impact of recent economic improvements on urban conditions such as hunger and homeless "has had very little positive impact."[1]

Michigan Governor John Engler, a welfare reform pioneer among governors, states, "A rising tide should lift all boats, but after an unprecedented period of economic growth, many in our urban centers remain moored to shore. Our inner city poor live in a separate nation, and the few ties that bind them to the rest of us are growing more strained every day."[2]

With the welfare state in retreat and economic growth bypassing many pockets of urban destitution, the real question before us concerns what the present capacity is of the nongovernmental sector to improve conditions for low-income families. There is the real possibility that even the widespread social renewal described here will also largely bypass America's neediest citizens if additional steps are not taken to dramatically strengthen those neighborhood-based groups which are uniquely positioned to directly reach them.

For one thing, there is no guarantee that the large intergenerational transfer of wealth cited in chapter one will go to charitable giving, as opposed to direct personal spending or other forms of investment. Substantial portions of the inheritance may simply go into the stock market or to the purchase of vacation homes, yachts, and luxury cars.

Second, even if a higher portion of the inherited wealth income is directed to charity, there is no assurance that it will be directed to those programs that directly serve poor individuals, such as homeless programs, soup kitchens, housing-rehab programs, and so on, commonly referred to as human service programs.

The nonprofit social sector is vast, consisting of hospitals, theaters, colleges and universities, research, and civic organizations, each of which represents important and valued work, but which generally serves the middle and even upper classes.

Finally, even if charitable giving for private sector services to low-income families increases, there is no guarantee under existing policies that those added resources will be directed to many of the small-scale, innovative programs that are credited with being most effective at transforming the lives of those in need. Some of the most effective charities are very small, often faith-based programs that exist in neighborhood storefronts and churches.

Many of these programs are attempting to pick up the slack where welfare has retreated. Just how robust the civic sector presently is, or what its future prospects are, within low-income communities is a matter of vigorous debate. The assumption among many is that civil society can rebound fairly well in poorer communities, largely on its own, and rise to meet the challenge. For others, the assumption is that even if government directly undermined civil society, which most acknowledge it did to some extent, government's retreat does not ensure civil society's return. As Dan Coats, former senator and current ambassador to Germany, has said, "Getting government out of our lives will not *ipso facto* lead to a rebirth of private and civic virtue."[3] What is needed, he adds, is a policy that combines boldness with humility and realism in this area.

Whatever one's views regarding the cause of declining community in low-income neighborhoods—whether the cause is the welfare state, loss of jobs, the rise of pathology, or a combination of those factors—the question remains: what can be offered as an alternative to the welfare state?

Some recommend more volunteering. Politicians and other public leaders who support volunteerism regularly cite the statistic that nearly 110 million Americans volunteer 20 billion hours of their time annually—an average of 182 hours per person. Despite dire warnings of Americans "bowling alone," the evidence seems to suggest that this form of civic engagement remains rather robust, as policymakers are quick to point out.

But, once again, one must look candidly at the limits of this remedy. Much of current volunteering, for example, is not provided in the form of human services, the area of greatest concern to us here. In fact, only 9.5 percent of those 110 million volunteers work in such human service fields as helping the homeless.[4] The vast majority of volunteerism consists of involvement in one's church, bake sales for the local school, serving on community boards, and so on. Even in churches, a very small percentage—15 percent—of volunteering goes beyond sanctuary walls.[5]

With great regularity, individuals volunteer for Habitat for Humanity projects, food and clothing distribution, and numerous forms of mentoring, and this should, of course, be encouraged. Moreover, there is much that suburban churches and middle-class civic groups can do to partner with effective urban programs, and it is important that better use be made of these partnerships.

But middle-class volunteerism, however well-intentioned and even effective, is hardly a sufficient answer to persistent urban poverty. Providing continuous and personal care, the qualities that most strongly commend private religious charity, is rarely supplied by the casual or occasional volunteer.

Others cite the remarkable level of current charitable giving in America as evidence that the private sector is ready to step forward and confront poverty. But general reliance on private charitable giving, as important as it is, does not go far enough either. Like the distribution of American volunteer activity, private charitable giving may have to be expanded dramatically—and more importantly redirected—in order to fill the gap in social services.

Of the $203 billion given to charity, 36.5 percent goes to religious organizations, 13.8 percent to educational organizations, 9.3 percent to health organizations, and only 8.8 percent to social service organizations (even though the number of nonprofit organizations providing social services comprise approximately 40 percent of the whole).[6]

Targeting Assistance

New efforts to expand the role of private charity must target assistance where it is needed the most. Improving the well-being of low-income families is not going to be accomplished through casual volunteers from distant places or through more generous charitable giving to schools, museums, hospitals, or churches which overwhelmingly serve the nonpoor.

Where resources need to be directed are to the local neighborhood renewal workers that neighborhood renewal activist Bob Woodson calls the "Josephs," those "embers of health and restoration" that often produce dramatic results on meager resources, whether in controlling gangs, curing addictions, or curbing poverty. What is unique about these local neighborhood renewal activities is their location: they take place in underserved communities, day and night, acting as antibodies against social viruses. They are an organic part of the community, not periodic visitors. They share the same zip code as the problem they are attempting to confront, as Woodson describes it.[7]

There was a time not long ago when these local charities labored in obscurity to all but a small group of local admirers and an even smaller group of national self-help advocates who saw in what they are accomplishing is a glimpse of the future. Recently, these local antipoverty activists have made their way to the center stage of America's social policy debate. The reason for their sudden emergence is their unusually high effectiveness in dealing with a range of problems, from drug addiction, to family breakup, to welfare dependency.

It is important not only to acknowledge their effectiveness, but to identify with some precision the reasons for it. Private and community-based programs are praised for being personal, challenging, flexible, innovative, community-centered, results-driven, and often spiritually renewing. In contrast, government programs are seen as undemanding, rule-bound, distant, unaccountable, impersonal, and hyper-secular.[8]

This more recent shift to policies of personal responsibilities, according to poverty expert Joel Schwartz, "returns us to the strategy of nineteenth century American moral reformers, who attempted to make the poor less poor by making them more virtuous." Charity campaigns in that century sought to effect moral reformation and self-discipline. In exchange for society's help, individuals living in poverty bore an obligation to better themselves. According to Schwartz, reformers at the time argued "that society should enable the poor to help themselves, and contended that the latter could so by practicing humble virtues such as diligence, sobriety, thrift, and familial responsibility."[9]

These personal factors are held by the vast majority of poverty researchers and workers today to be irrelevant at best, and at worst tantamount to "blaming the victim," a phrase which itself signals the modern shift from personal responsibility to victimization. To be fair, the degree to which individuals in poverty hold some responsibility for their plight is a deeply philosophical and even theological debate of long standing. That the urban poor today have suffered from profound economic dislocation associated with the collapse of an urban manufacturing economy, there can be no doubt. Still, the evidence also suggests that many low-income and unemployed persons have compounded their plight by turning away from the ethic of self-reliance and industry that enabled the poor of the past to, over time, conquer disadvantages and injustices.

Wherever one settles on this philosophical divide, it appears that all sides in the debate are to varying degrees extending fresh support to faith-based charities, and often for the reason that they are able to treat the whole person: body, mind, and spirit. The providers of care typically suffer with and are in relationship to struggling individuals in a manner that is personal and continuous. With this approach, givers of care treat struggling individuals, not as clients, but as persons who were made in the image and likeness of God and who thus bear inherent dignity and worth. And this, it is too infrequently noted, is good for the moral health of the caregiver, the volunteer, and the donor. Acts of sacrifice and mutual assistance redound to the benefit of those performing such acts, not to mention to the community as a whole.

Much like nineteenth-century charities that were less affected by the secularizing, bureaucratizing forces of modernity, these local charities understand that the problems of idleness, drunkenness, crime, and promiscuity cannot be separated from issues of moral culture and private character. Although the nineteenth century offers important lessons for today in delivering effective charity, most acknowledge that the circumstances of the late twentieth century are radically different from those of the late nineteenth century. Modern values and systems with their emphasis on secularism, compartmentalization, and professional specialization are pervasive, and will not be easily or rapidly thrown off.

Generating New Social Capital

While the remarkable stories of these small, local, church-affiliated charities are cited almost every day, there is little evidence to suggest that their successes can be replicated on a large scale without some attempt to widen their support base. These once obscure charities are now carrying expectations that may be impossible for most of them to meet under existing circumstances. As Reverend Eugene Rivers of Boston has said: "Without public support and back-up, financial and logistical, there's no way churches or other community folk can turn the tide."[10]

The charities we celebrate the most for their effectiveness are working their miracles in the midst of the most concentrated and intractable poverty. Many needy Americans have a legitimate claim on society's compassion, but especially those who occupy our urban pockets of poverty. The number of people living in high-poverty neighborhoods almost doubled since 1970. Eight million people, nearly a third of them children, now live in neighborhoods where more than 40 percent of residents are poor, and many more subsist on low-wage jobs.

They operate in communities where material resources are very scarce and civic institutions have withered to the point of near extinction. In many cases, these churches and faith-based charities are the last remaining line of defense against complete civic collapse. Says national expert John DiIulio of the University of Pennsylvania, "churches are clearly the ideal—indeed, in most cases, the only—mediating institutions in black inner-city neighborhoods." DiIulio cites studies indicating that 70 percent of urban black congregations run or participate directly in community outreach activities—staffing day care facilities, offering drug- and alcohol-abuse prevention programs, administering food banks, building shelters, serving and safe havens, and more.[11]

It is worth pondering what a huge burden would suddenly be transferred to already weak municipal governments in these areas if churches, synagogues, and mosques suddenly stopped doing the work they are doing. It is also worth imagining what might be achieved in our cities if we could double, triple, or quadruple the work these religious institutions are doing. If America is going to have a true antipoverty strategy, it must dramatically expand this civic capacity in high-poverty neighborhoods.

The support from within these communities is very limited, and the source of potential support that lies beyond these communities, such as foundations and corporations, is either unavailable or problematic. The answer may not be in lecturing corporations to do more, because what they already do with their money is too frequently misguided. For one, major corporations and the largely secular charities they typically support frequently run on the same premises as government and are thus often no more effective. Much of this corporate philanthropy is guided more by what is thought to be politically fashionable than by any criteria of effectiveness.

If this is the approach that is taken by turning to the private sector to replace government, "we could end up with a welfare regime just as dysfunctional as the one we are struggling to replace," maintains James Payne. Typically, this form of private charity is most likely to practice "sympathetic giving," which is as indiscriminate as government welfare, and can be just as counterproductive.[12]

Similarly, major corporations often shy away from assisting organizations that are religious in nature. However, there is evidence of some recent softening of attitudes here, for example, in support for such programs as the Jeremiah Project, headed by DiIulio, which is targeting corporations for greater involvement in the faith-based social service sector.

In spite of small changes in this area recently, it remains doubtful that funding small religious charities will suddenly become the hottest trend in corporate philanthropy, and even if it should, corporate contributions represent only 5.6 percent of philanthropic giving in America, compared to nearly 80 percent that comes from individuals.[13]

If civil society in most low-income communities is in various degrees of extinction, and if the private sector remedies currently being offered—middle class volunteerism and corporate philanthropy—are not sufficient, what should public policy do to help invigorate low-income communities?

That we need increased capacity for local, indigenous, effective charities, there should be no doubt. But there are any number of ways to expand the capacity, not all of which are equally ideal. The central question becomes: what public policy is most effective, and most consistent with the nonbureaucratic nature of the civil society enterprise?

Local Government Support

One approach is to simply encourage state and local governments to more consciously support local charities as part of their antipoverty programming. Indeed, according to Joe Loconte, "massive, direct public funding for private nonprofits is quickly becoming the most important strategy for attacking social problems in America." "Countless charities and other nonprofits," he says, "are now heavily subsidized to deliver care; many of these 'private' groups depend on public funds for well over half of their income," a trend he finds worrisome.[14]

The practice of directly supporting charities through local government has a long history. Local government support for charity was not uncommon throughout American history, even during periods when private church-based programs made up the bulk of local charity. Except perhaps during colonial America, charity was never the exclusive province of the private sector. For example, private charities for poor children operating in New York in the 1870s received half of their funding from state and local governments. But this practice becomes vastly more complex and problematic in today's environment in which the government has a way of controlling what it touches. In fact, thanks to a vast array of statutes that did not exist even thirty years ago, the government has no choice today but to assert controls over the activity it funds.

The state is capable not only of preempting private local charity by replacing local caregivers with social service professionals, as mentioned earlier, it can deform these charities by suffocating them with direct grants, procedures, and various regulations. It would be a shame if, in our rush to see effective local charities flourish, we fall back on a common American habit of merely throwing money at them, which could result in undermining their effectiveness through what Loconte calls "mission creep."

The Charitable Tax Credit

While it would be foolish to think that local charities do not need greater capacity, as has been indicated here, it would be just as foolhardy to underestimate the capacity of public policy to weaken their effectiveness. So the real question becomes *how* can we help? Expanding the use of the charitable tax credit has merit as a capacity builder for several equally important reasons.

One, it preserves the entrepreneurial qualities that made local charities effective in the first place. Local nonprofit charities are famous for their entrepreneurial verve in selling their programming to local donors, and have little experience drafting proposals for government agencies. It is not uncommon for local charities which suddenly come upon state money to spend days and even weeks receiving new training in how to satisfy government bureaucrats.

Suddenly program "outcomes" become measured, not in saved lives, but in how well charity workers have performed in the great paper chase. Loconte writes, "With government grants and contracts come government standards—reams of regulations intended to ensure accountability and guarantee quality care. What they guarantee instead is mind boggling waste."[15]

When the means of organizing a local charity involves going directly to local supporters, the voluntary nature of this activity is preserved.

Two, because the charitable tax credit would not involve transfers from the taxpayer to the charitable recipient via the government, it would neither waste money through needless administrative overhead, nor produce a whole new layer of middlemen, including government workers, lobbyists, and grant-making consultants. Government grant-making to local social agencies invariably ends up expanding the class of people whose employment consists, not in serving low-income families, but in lobbying, writing grants, conducting or attending conferences, and engaging in political advocacy.

Three, the charitable tax credit goes the farthest in protecting the autonomy of the charitable entity from state encroachment. What the government funds, it will regulate for the sake of public accountability. It would be derelict of a funding agency not to impose some programming controls to ensure that public purposes are being served and to guard against gross inefficiencies or outright abuse of public money.

Four, and directly related to three, the charitable tax credit is the most viable arrangement for supporting the important but too-frequently underestimated work that religious institutions and agencies perform. Thanks to public officials' sudden rediscovery of faith-based charities, our social policy has made significant shifts in new directions. For example, poverty is now viewed less as a material condition, and more as a condition requiring personal and spiritual care. Many, including traditional defenders of the welfare state, now admit to the impoverishing effects of secular, systemically impersonal bureaucracies on families struggling in poverty. Publicly employed social service professionals are rarely prepared, even if authorized, to care for the souls of the people they serve or to treat them as whole persons rather than as clients in search of a specific public service.

Faith-based institutions have a vital role to play in the renewal of America's communities. Most are aware of the mountain of evidence that confirms the healing and renewing powers of religious faith in all facets of life, for rich and poor alike, whether in marriage, work, or dealing with life's setbacks. Research shows that religious faith, like no other force, has a positive impact on a host of pathologies like drug abuse, alcoholism, and crime.[16] The charitable tax credit is a promising tool in the ongoing effort to expand the vital work of faith-based organizations.

Five, the charitable tax credit enhances more active and generous citizenship on the part of the supporting public. When state funding accounts for 60 percent or more of a nonprofit service provider's budget, more is lost than the charity's independence and voluntary character. Members of the public are more likely to be denied an opportunity to participate in local problem solving—through their dollars, their active concern and prayers, and in many cases their personal participation. The more opportunities we give to ordinary citizens, volunteers, and nonprofit entrepreneurs to perform publicly important work, the better our society's overall condition will be.

If corporations and secular grant-making foundations are cool toward religious charity, individual Americans themselves are decidedly warm toward them. According to a Gallup poll, 58 percent of all Americans, and an astonishing 86 percent of black Americans, believe that religion, churches, or faith-based organizations can help solve contemporary social problems.[17]

Supplanting individual giving with state taxing, granting, and oversight activity undermines the civic heritage. For our democratic system to flourish, we must do all we can to reinforce the "we-the-people" mentality which holds up local self-government as a democratic imperative.

Six, the final and most compelling reason for adopting the charitable tax credit as the preferred means of directing badly needed aid to low-income communities is, quite simply, this is where the money is. Individual Americans are the world's foremost contributors to private charities, with average middle-class Americans contributing far more than the rich, and the poorest Americans giving the highest percentage of their incomes. Nearly 75 percent of U.S. households report some contribution, with 90 percent of all giving taking place locally.[18]

Several states have passed a charity tax credit or have legislation under active consideration. The Arizona state legislature passed a bill to provide a 100 percent credit for contributions to charities which assist low-income individuals, with a ceiling of $100 per person, $200 for couples. In Pennsylvania, a bill to provide a 50 percent credit on contributions to qualified charities is under active consideration in both chambers. Similar proposals are under consideration in Indiana, Minnesota, and North Carolina.

There are difficulties to be overcome in more widely applying the charitable tax credit at the state level, to be sure. For example, policy analysts are finding it challenging to develop acceptable criteria for the activities to which the credit should be applied. Each of the pending bills makes its own attempt to limit the tax credit to "qualified" activity. For example, the Indiana bill applies the credit to contributions that have been made to organizations serving individuals at no more than 185 percent of the federal poverty rate, and to specific antipoverty services such as housing, emergency shelters, job training services, substance abuse services, soup kitchens, and food banks.

A second drawback to the charitable tax credit is figuring out how to implement it in states that have no individual income tax. One suggested alternative for such states is to provide a rebate to qualified individual contributors.

These limits notwithstanding, the charitable tax credit is emerging as a key tool in the movement to renew civil society in America. Of its many advantages, all enumerated above, the leading advantage is its capacity to tap into the expanding resources of individual middle-class givers in order to empower those neighborhood charities that are on the frontlines of fighting inner city poverty.

Notes

1. Arianna Huffington, "Grandstanding and the Homeless," *Washington Times*, January 4, 1999.

2. John Engler and Bill Shuette, "Urban Homesteading—An Urban Policy for a New Century," *American Outlook* (Spring 1998): 60.

3. William J. Bennett and Dan Coats, "Moving Beyond Devolution," *Wall Street Journal*, August 15, 1995.

4. *Giving and Volunteering in the United States* (Washington, D.C.: Independent Sector, 1999).

5. Michael J. Gerson, "Do Do-Gooders Do Much Good?," *U.S. News & World Report* (April 29, 1997): 27.

6. *Giving USA 2001* (Indianapolis: American Association for Fundraising Counsel, 2001), and Susan Gray, "Americans' Gifts Top $150 Billion," *Chronicle of Philanthropy* (June 12, 1997), 41.

7. See Robert L. Woodson Sr., *The Triumphs of Joseph: How Today's Community Healers Are Reviving Our Streets and Neighborhoods* (New York: Free Press, 1998).

8. Bennett and Coats, "Moving Beyond Devolution."

9. Joel Schwartz, "Poverty and Moral Renaissance," *American Outlook* (Spring 1998): 62.

10. Gerson, "Do Do-Gooders Do Much Good?," 27.

11. John DiIulio, Jr. "The Coming of the Super-Preachers," *Weekly Standard* (June 23, 1997): 24.

12. James L. Payne, "The Smart Samaritan," *Policy Review* (May-June 1997): 49.

13. Gray, "Americans' Gifts," 41.

14. Joe Loconte, "The Seven Deadly Sins of Government Funding," *Policy Review* (March-April 1997): 28.

15. Loconte, "The Seven Deadly Sins," 29.

16. Joseph P. Shapiro and Andrea R. Wright, "Can Churches Cure America's Social Ills?" *U.S. News and World Report*, September 9, 1996, 50.

17. DiIulio, "The Coming of the Super-Preachers," 24.

18. Geneva Overholser, "Let The Giving Grow," *Washington Post*, February 10, 1999, A23.

Chapter Six

A Humane Economy
The Moral Dimensions of Enterprise

Ryan Streeter

In 1520 Charles V, emperor of the Holy Roman Empire, was on his way to visit Antwerp, Belgium. In anticipation of his entrance into the city, residents and city leaders decorated the roadway with a variety of tableaux carved out of wood. The tableaux typically cast culturally important themes and principles in pictorial form. One of the pictures showed Philologia (learning) and Mercury (commerce) triumphing over representations of Ignorance and Barbarism.[1]

Already in the early sixteenth century, commercial centers such as Antwerp were realizing that countries with market economies were more successful at refining the manners of citizens than countries that relied solely on political power to keep order. If learning, or Philologia, could conquer Ignorance, then commerce, or Mercury, could conquer Barbarism. The antidote to a superstitious and unlearned generation was a strong university culture. The antidote to uncultivated and barbaric manners was the market.

Already in commercially sophisticated, early modern societies, people understood that activities such as buying and selling, producing and pricing, manufacturing and trading, kept people preoccupied and prevented them from taking out their aggression on each other or through politically violent means. The emerging market economy was a moral force. It channeled aggression to productive activity and relied upon good sense, hard work, delayed gratification, and compromise. Its early proponents recognized this. They began to regard market activity as one of the strongest humanizing forces available to political regimes.

Today, countries with the freest markets enjoy an absence of the inhumanity found in countries that are not economically liberal. The Index of Economic Freedom, co-published by the *Wall Street Journal* and the Heritage Foundation, shows that countries with high degrees of economic freedom not only benefit from stronger long-term economic growth than countries enjoying less economic freedom, but they are also marked by much higher levels of civility and tolerance. In economically "un-free" countries, the authors write, "hopelessness and isolation foment fanaticism and terrorism."[2] In these nations, the barbarians rule, and Mercury is held in chains.

While this evidence of the viability of economic freedom would gratify the early moderns' confidence in commerce, were they able to address us today, these pioneers of wealth and markets would warn us about something else: our general belief that character-forming institutions and market institutions have little to do with one another. They never believed that the market could be the sole and chief civilizing force in a society.

The most famous and influential economic theorist of the eighteenth century, Adam Smith, was a professor of moral philosophy. Like most of his contemporaries, Smith was greatly concerned about the effect of commerce on character. While commerce possessed a humanizing force of its own by teaching people the value of saving and hard work, it also threatened to let avarice become our ruling passion. Commerce's actors, it was widely believed, had to be continually fed by moral sources outside the market. We are all in need of the "good company," Smith wrote, which is found in families, neighbors, and communities and in which "justice, modesty, humanity, and good order" are learned.[3] Smith and his contemporaries believed that commerce could not risk being separated from the moral wellsprings of human association, which equip us with a sympathy for others strong enough to keep avarice in check.

The Sectored Economy

The view that there exists a positive relationship between civility and economic health has been largely undermined. Throughout the twentieth century, a good many public intellectuals and academics saw no necessary connection between economic liberty and what the German economist Wilhelm Röpke called "political and spiritual freedom." Recounting a conversation with Benedetto Croce, known as one of the most formidable European intellects of the twentieth century, Röpke explains how Croce justified his support of collectivist economic systems. Only political and spiritual freedom mattered to Croce, who said that "economic freedom belonged to a lower and independent sphere" in which "the only question was one of expediency in the manner of organizing our economic life, and this question was not to be related with the decisive and incomparably higher question of political and spiritual freedom."[4] Croce was merely expressing a view that had widely taken root in both the United States and Europe: the market is morally inert and unrelated to questions of moral, spiritual, and political well-being.

Concurrent with the spread of this view throughout elite strata of American society, the market grew more and more independent organizationally. The U.S.

Department of Commerce's national income accounts created "sectors" after World War II. Separate from business and government, the "nonprofit sector" was invented as the domain in which most morally and spiritually significant activity takes place. The intersection between market forces and social purposes has become increasingly difficult to descry.

The marketplace is rarely conceived as a place in which social ailments can be effectively confronted. Its most successful members are often overlooked by community leaders who would never consider involving them in the struggle against homelessness, joblessness, child poverty, and other problems. They may be asked to serve on nonprofit boards and to contribute money to social causes, but they are rarely asked to join their entrepreneurial talents and existing enterprises in creative responses to critical needs. Nonprofit leaders have accepted their sectored fate and rely upon their own nonprofit networks and associations, foundation funding, and perhaps an occasional public grant to craft solutions on their own. The social sector, it is commonly believed, exists to take on social problems. The market is something else.

Our strong market economy may create conditions that foster basic civility, but we have to ask ourselves what we lose by separating our moral and social concerns from our market realities. In practice, we seem to have bought the view that the market is nothing but the harsh arena in which self-interested people do battle for profits, while the humane part of human nature expresses itself through not-for-profit activity.

The Roots of a Humane Economy

Röpke wrote that "the prosaic world of business draws on ethical reserves by which it stands and falls and which are more important than economic laws and principles."[5] It is only in preserving the links between the sources of these "ethical reserves" and business practices that we can have a "humane economy," according to this illustrious but largely forgotten economist. He writes:

> Self-discipline, a sense of justice, honesty, fairness, chivalry, moderation, public spirit, respect for human dignity, firm ethical norms—all of these are things which people must possess before they go to market and compete with each other. These are the indispensable supports which preserve both market and competition from degeneration. Family, church, genuine communities, and tradition are their sources. It is also necessary that people should grow up in conditions which favor such moral convictions, conditions of a natural order, conditions promoting cooperation, respecting tradition, and giving moral support to the individual.[6]

Röpke was a well-known skeptic of a centralized government's ability to preserve the integrity of civil society, but he also considered unguarded, laissez-faire market activity as a threat to our moral and social stability. He called the individual's sense of responsibility "the secret mainspring of society," which large welfare states undermine. Likewise, the "cult of the standard of living," as he preferred to call it, leads to a "misjudgment of the true scale of vital values" when it runs amok and becomes an all-consuming society unto itself, separate from the humanizing forces of family, faith, and community.[7]

It is only by preserving a connection between the humane sentiments most likely to be found in the institutions of civil society, or the social sector, and the engines of commerce and market vitality that a healthy societal balance is achieved. This balance is important, for the principles and habits of each make the other stronger the more they can inform and play off one another. Röpke has said that "we need a combination of supreme moral sensitivity and economic knowledge. Economically ignorant moralism is as objectionable as morally callous economism."[8] And just as moral sensitivity needs to be refined by the calculating reason of economics, so too does economic thought and activity need "humane values."[9]

In our sectored society, we assign "social problems" to our nonprofit organizations, foundations, and public agencies, which are rooted in principled moral commitments, at least in their origins if not in their present conceptions of themselves. But they are too often "economically ignorant." Likewise, by relieving market institutions and actors of any serious moral commitments as they fulfill their assignment to create wealth, we make "moral callousness" an easy prospect.

The question, then, remains: to whom do we turn to preserve, or create, this connection between the world of humane values and market life? The answer Röpke gives is twofold, and it applies to us today. Instead of turning to government or a multisector task force or celebrity spokespeople, we should first look to those who are already leading on this front in their communities and in public life. This is the first point. Look to the exemplary among you, Röpke says, who have committed themselves to a "life of dedicated endeavor on behalf of all, unimpeachable integrity, constant restraint of our common greed, proved soundness of judgment, a spotless private life, indomitable courage in standing up for truth and law, and generally the highest example."[10]

Röpke, who fled the Germany he loved after receiving threats for speaking out against National Socialism early in Hitler's rise to power, calls such leaders a "moral aristocracy," a kind of "natural nobility"—an obvious riposte to the perverted racial aristocracy envisioned by the Nazis. Moral aristocrats rise to leadership status not by their race or class or anything other than their moral habits and judgments. The "ultimate fate of the market economy," Röpke says, depends on whether these are "people who, by position and conviction, have close ties to the market economy and who feel responsible for it in the moral sphere."[11]

These individuals cannot work in isolation, however, and this is the second point. We must also have a society rich in "independent institutions . . . possessing the authority of guardians of universal and lasting values which cannot be bought."[12] These are the institutions of civil society such as churches and foundations as well as, Röpke says, other social and economic stabilizing forces such as the judiciary and the central banks. While not all of our present-day "independent institutions" are the guardians Röpke envisioned, we clearly have an uncontestably strong civil society on which the moral exemplars among us—those who "feel responsible for the economy in the moral sphere"—can draw.

Prospects for a Humane Economy

Obviously, the effects of a sectored economy are larger than any single initiative, program, or idea can confront. Bringing the energy and innovation of business together with the compassion and care of the social sector will not happen by a natural course of events or simple historical accident. It requires moral imagination and the willful creativity of social entrepreneurs.

It is tempting to think in grand terms and to suggest that high-level, structural reforms are necessary to bring social mission and market realities into better cooperation. However, it is easy to idealize large-scale reforms—whether they are right-leaning proposals to marketize the social sector or left-leaning proposals to socialize the market sector—and ignore smaller-scale, local innovations. An economy is only as humane as the practices of the people involved. While large-scale reforms have their proper place, we can begin our pursuit of a humane economy by fostering a culture of social entrepreneurship on the ground, in our communities, in our boardrooms. It is at this level that the institutions of civil society can work with the world of business to effect substantial and positive change.

In particular, activity is needed in two areas. First, we should be watchful for opportunities in which business interests and social needs are served in one and the same enterprise. Second, we would do well to ask those who have succeeded in their adventures in the marketplace to apply their talents, resources, and abilities to successful social ventures. This work does not need to be created from scratch. There already exist a wide variety of individuals and organizations in America that have combined market success with social purpose, and we can learn from them.

Social Enterprise

Across America one can find a variety of strategies for working with market realities and institutions to achieve socially redeeming purposes. These can loosely be collected under the rubric "social enterprise." Social enterprise refers not to the mere implementation of higher codes of ethics or more humane practices in the internal processes of a business, but the actual, external relationship of a business enterprise with organizations, people, and objectives in the social sector. A business enterprise may be a regular for-profit company or a nonprofit organization that runs a business enterprise. The following are examples of particularly promising social enterprises.

The Connector. The Jobs Partnership of Raleigh, North Carolina, connects unconventional partners: businesses and inner-city churches. The organization was formed in 1996 by a Raleigh businessman, Chris Mangum, and an urban pastor, Reverend Donald McCoy, as a solution to a two-pronged practical problem: Mangum's company needed workers, and McCoy's congregation had members in need of work. They expanded their partnership by inviting area businesses and churches to join them in bringing jobs to the jobless. These unconventional partners were so successful that they attracted the attention of people across the nation. There are now Jobs Partnerships in twenty-five cities throughout the United States and altogether, in just five years, Jobs Partnerships have served more than 1,200 clients nationwide.

The Jobs Partnership holds twelve-week courses for prospective workers and offers a personalized job placement service in partnership with participating businesses. The courses, usually held in one of the churches, are framed by a biblical worldview, and they cover everything from job skills to life skills to discovering a sense of purpose, vocational and otherwise. Once a student completes the course, he or she searches a database of available employment positions, posted by participating companies. Once a match is made, students are ensconced in a culture of support as they transition onto their newfound vocational path. They have church-based mentors, and the businesses provide a "buddy" to help the new employees find their way on the job. Nearly 85 percent of the individuals that have gone through the program nationwide have remained employed and productive.

The Jobs Partnership's unique role as connector produces results in several ways. More than 70 percent of the partnership's clients in Raleigh earn between 13 and 100 percent more than the average client of North Carolina's welfare to work program.[13] The participating companies report a high level of satisfaction with Jobs Partnership graduates, citing the employees' work preparedness and ongoing culture of support as main reasons. And, finally, the Jobs Partnership has been a catalyst in breaking down barriers between the largely white suburban business community and the largely African American inner-city church community.

The Jobs Partnership offers a concrete example of how a "connector organization" can serve business and social interests at the same time. Because all parties' interests are served well, results follow, and the public good is strengthened. Similar opportunities for social entrepreneurs exist across the nation for grassroots organizations with personal connections to individuals in need of a vocation and businesses in need of workers.

Business Catalyst. ARAMARK ServiceMaster Facility Services, a multi-billion-dollar food, facility, and uniform services company, operates a Work Training Businesses division with the objective of helping nonprofit human services organizations start and run businesses that employ hard-to-serve individuals. The nonprofit organization outsources various aspects of employee training and management as well as client contract management to ARAMARK ServiceMaster. Typically, the Work Training Businesses are run by homeless shelters in mid-size to large cities.

The benefit to the shelters is essentially twofold. They can add services with the additional revenue generated by the business, unlike revenue from grants and government programs, which must usually be used for carefully defined purposes. And they can help their clients transition toward self-sufficiency by having a business but without having to build up the business administrative capacity in-house.

The benefit to ARAMARK ServiceMaster is threefold, according to Bill Bedrossian, chief operating officer of the Work Training Businesses. For one thing, the training businesses build upon and grow a core service of the corporation: management services. Second, with the development of people as a key ARAMARK ServiceMaster mission, the training businesses create an expanded labor pool out of the "graduates" of the businesses. The workers in the businesses are "a day away from being employees in our other standard businesses," Bedrossian remarks. And third, the training businesses build strong relationships in the communities where they work. Nonprofit organizations boards and public agencies provide extended networks of opportunity.

The Work Training Businesses have the potential for impressive growth. For example, between 1993 and 2001, ServiceMaster helped the Chicago Christian Industrial League, a century-old homeless shelter, build a landscaping business from a $330,000 business to a $3.5 million operation that tended to some of Chicago's most visible greenspaces. The business grew to account for half of the organization's total revenue, thus granting it the freedom to offer its client population a variety of services for which it previously had no budget. ServiceMaster, in turn, gained a productive business partnership, access to a new market by working with its inner-city partner, and it has trained more than 1000 people for employment in the business.

One of ServiceMaster's core principles is that developing people goes hand in hand with building a successful enterprise. Bedrossian says that the corporation's partnerships with nonprofit human services organizations is an extension of this principle. Rather than regarding a homeless shelter's client base as a high-need, at-risk population to be sequestered away from the rest of society, Bedrossian sees an opportunity to develop productive employees of a productive business.

Full-fledged Social Enterprise. Seattle-based Pioneer Human Services is perhaps the largest and most dynamic example of how a business enterprise can serve social needs for which we usually create separate social sector programs and organizations. Begun in 1962 to serve at-risk youth, Pioneer began experimenting with business management in 1984. At the time, it was a $4 million nonprofit organization with three-quarters of its revenue coming from government grants. It is now a $55 million nonprofit organization wholly self-dependent on the revenue it generates from its numerous enterprises that employ chronically unemployed individuals, recovering drug and alcohol abusers, and others facing serious challenges to work and self-reliance.

Pioneer operates an enterprise that manufactures light-metal parts for everything from aircraft to medical equipment. It has a distribution service with three business units, a food service, a warehousing service, and more. It even operates the café in the Starbucks Coffee Company's Seattle headquarters. Altogether, Pioneer serves more than 6,000 people annually and employs 1,000. It provides a range of supportive, housing, and other services to the people that come through its doors. Through and through, it is an organization committed to the improvement of the lives of people on the margins of society.

Gary Mulhair, the visionary leader who transformed Pioneer into the enterprise-based organization it is today, sees an opportunity for corporations to support social enterprises. Instead of engaging in "strategic philanthropy," the term typically used to describe corporate philanthropy that serves corporate interests, Mulhair advocates "operationalized philanthropy." He says, "Instead of giving us money, give us work. We'll convert that to jobs and hire people you won't hire. You'll receive products and services you need at a competitive price."[14] Organizations like Pioneer provide corporations with competent business partners who also serve highly important social purposes.

Social Enterprise Investor. The Roberts Enterprise Development Fund (REDF) in San Francisco is a foundation acting as a venture capitalist for social-purpose enterprises in the Bay Area. Its portfolio of "investees" consists of nonprofit organizations running businesses that employ diverse populations of disadvantaged youth, homeless individuals, and people suffering from psychiatric disabilities. REDF, unlike conventional foundations, does not give out grants; it makes investments. It invests money into nonprofit enterprises in order to build organizational infrastructure and strategic business development. It pays for business assistants to help the enterprises run like businesses, and it provides the organizations with access to Bay Area business networks. In short, its disbursements to its portfolio organizations are intended to increase the self-sustainability and productivity of the organizations.

REDF's hallmark innovation is its "social return on investment" metric (SROI). The SROI calculates the public savings and new taxes generated when a portfolio enterprise's employees leave publicly funded services for employment. It also tracks conventional enterprise financials, such as sales and margins, as well as a variety of social impact indicators such as housing status to self-esteem levels. Together, the various return on investment metrics form a blended index of return, which essentially represents the total value (economic and social) of the enterprise.[15]

REDF's approach to philanthropic giving, namely investing in the capacity of organizations, and its commitment to SROI betray a simple philosophy: results matter for people as well as business. REDF applies a market sector model to its own operation as a "social venture capitalist" and to its portfolio enterprises as a way to quantify the value of positive human change. And the very fact that it operates the way that it does prompts the human services organizations in its portfolio to produce results through business.

From Upwardly Mobile to Socially Noble

It is growing increasingly important that discussions about the best use of accumulated wealth find their way into regular public discourse. For one thing, the next fifty years will see an amazing transfer of wealth as baby boomers, who are inheriting a stockpile of wealth from their own parents, begin to retire with sizable fortunes, the use of which remains to be seen. The best conservative estimates, as chapter one pointed out, place the amount of this wealth at $41 trillion, with $6 trillion available for philanthropic purposes, but it is truly difficult to estimate what exactly will happen with these resources.[16] We do know, though, that those with wealth account for a large portion of all giving. The 4.9 percent of families in America with a net worth of more than $1 million make 42 percent of all charitable gifts.[17] It is thus highly important that our society provide effective ways for our growing number of millionaires to deploy their philanthropic dollars.

Another important reason for heightening public discussion about wealth accumulation is that there are simply going to be more elderly people around for longer. The "golden years" of retirement are growing longer. According to Peter Drucker, current trends show that the proportion of older people will rise steeply over the next thirty years while, over the same period, they will be living longer and likely working into their mid-70s.[18]

We thus need to think not merely about how much money is going to be available for philanthropy and charity over the next several generations but how people with time, resources, and a civic heart can best serve their communities. There has been quite a bit of discussion, at least among academics, about how much money will really be available as boomers retire. This is an interesting but not particularly useful conversation. We need to be talking instead about strategies for helping people make the best use of the full range of their resources, especially those who have succeeded in the marketplace and are now looking for the best way to transfer their energy into service to the community.

The Success to Significance Movement: Bob Buford's Halftime Phenomenon. As more and more Americans live longer lives, it becomes increasingly important to reexamine conventional conceptions of the retirement years. Bob Buford, a successful Texas cable television pioneer, has created a movement among businessmen and women around the idea that the game of life consists of two halves. The first consists of the years in which people are primarily concentrated on achieving vocational success, and the second is devoted to achieving significance by giving back to the community. Rather than experiencing a midlife crisis, he argues, we ought to experience "half time," during which we plan our second half with the same level of intention and dedication that we apply to the first half.

Buford writes in *Halftime*, "The game is won or lost in the second half, not the first . . . . The first half of life has to do with getting and gaining, learning and earning . . . . The second half is more risky because it has to do with living beyond the immediate. It is about releasing the seed of creativity and energy that has been implanted within us" to produce meaningful change in the world, to give to others, to strengthen communities.[19] Giving back in the second half is best accomplished not merely by setting up a foundation and hiring professional staff to disburse money but by getting engaged and putting to use the same talents that have led to success in the first half of life.

To support and further the message of the book, Buford has started an organization, Halftime, which exposes people to a reconsideration of midlife decision-making and a reevaluation of retirement. His organization provides tools and services to assist people in moving "from success to significance" by helping them use their success-enabling talents and skills for lasting social sector change. Over the past decade, Buford has engaged thousands of individuals who find themselves at the crossroads of success and significance.

While Buford is motivated by a distinctively Christian worldview and his message is designed for a primarily Christian audience, as Peter Drucker writes in the preface to *Halftime*, the book has application to a wide and diverse audience. Drucker writes, "Whatever one's values and commitments—and they need not be at all those of Bob Buford—this book should be the catalyst for all those who are the beneficiaries of the two great social developments of this century: the extension of the life span (especially of the working life span), and the fact that it is now possible to be a 'success' and to make a life out of one's living."[20]

Drucker continues to argue that Buford's work holds important promise for the future of democracy in America. He says, "This is an important *political* book as well. We increasingly realize that modern government is not capable of taking care of community and social problems. Nor is the free market." We have to turn to the social sector, Drucker says, and especially to an enhanced reliance upon the citizenship of engaged volunteers. The importance of *Halftime*, he says, is that it points the way to a solution to "the major political challenge of a developed society: that middle-aged success can help restore the body politic to function, to effectiveness, and to a reaffirmation of the basic values of both democracy and community."[21] Clearly, given the changing demographics in America, a broader movement to equip and enable our aging population to convert their success into significance will strengthen the American project.

Turning Corporate Power into Civic Purpose: The Newark Alliance. Success can also turn into significance as leading members of the corporate world channel their influence toward civic purposes, especially when they do so collectively. The Newark Alliance is an example and model of this kind of collective force. Founded in 1999, its board is comprised of eight high-profile individuals such as the Amelior Foundation's Ray Chambers and Prudential Insurance's Arthur Ryan, and it is chaired by former Governor Thomas Kean. *Business News New Jersey* has called the Newark Alliance "one of the city's most influential nonprofits."[22]

The Alliance's aim is to improve the prosperity of New Jersey's largest city by improving its economic and educational environment. Funded by its board, the Alliance can stay focused on its mission without having to divert its energies into fundraising. It works closely with a range of public, private, and civic institutions, not in an attempt to construct new institutions or wide-sweeping panaceas to the area's problems, but to build upon existing resources, services, and community assets. It helps create new initiatives where they are needed but does so by bringing together the city's leading stakeholders and empowering them to create positive change.

Because it was founded primarily by corporate leaders who understand the business of strategic thinking, the Newark Alliance invests its resources and energies in ways that conventional community-building nonprofits might not. The Alliance's executive director, Dale Caldwell, a Princeton graduate with an M.B.A. from the Wharton School, is a former consultant with Deloitte and Touche. He routinely works with community leaders in strategic and tactical ways aimed at long-term productivity and improvement. He combines a deep commitment to social purposes with a long history of business sense and acumen.

For instance, he and his colleagues brought in consultants to help the Newark Public Schools correct and streamline its payroll processing, long a system plagued with incongruities, waste, and immense frustration. They also worked with consultants to refashion the strategic vision and operations of the Newark Economic Development Corporation, the city's chief development arm, so that it could proactively attract the kinds of investments the city would need to grow. These types of improvements are the work that is fundamental and necessary but which organizations are often unwilling to undertake or unable to do for lack of skill and knowledge. The Newark Alliance combines high-level influence with problem-solving that works through strategic thinking rather than simply by "putting out fires," a long-standing characteristic of social sector organizations.

High-Level Human Capital: New York City Investment Fund. If Halftime is a call to successful individuals to pursue significance, and if the Newark Alliance is an example of how successful corporate leaders can band together for civic purposes, the New York City Investment Fund is a model of collective corporate investment in socially beneficial business ventures. That is, it is a model of investment in business enterprises that address important civic and social needs in New York City. The New York City Investment Fund consists of twenty-eight board members, all of whom are high-level corporate leaders and CEOs and none of whom are public officials. While corporate leaders have come together in a number of American cities for more than fifty years to form funds aimed at addressing important social needs, they have rarely been as directly engaged as the New York City Investment Fund's board members.[23]

The Fund has more than $100 million under management. Since its founding in 1996, it has invested $50 million in forty-seven different projects. These projects range from Internet start-ups to retailers to entertainment companies to health care organizations to computer recycling plants, most of which serve a distinct social purpose such as creating jobs for marginalized minorities or providing health care services for the underserved. To date, the funded projects have created nearly 3,000 new jobs in New York City.[24] "The Fund is neither a profit-maximizing venture-capital company nor a social-change philanthropy, but draws on the perspective and know-how of both worlds," write Peter Plastrik and Kathryn Wylde.[25] It brings the power and resourcefulness of the market to social problems, and it infuses the moral substance of the social sector into market activity.

While the Fund's financial capital is important, its most important factor is its high-level human capital: the network of relationships represented by its board members, investors, and other individuals who volunteer time and talents to make the Fund's investments return real results. When he founded the Fund, Henry Kravis of the famous Kravis, Kohlberg, and Roberts leveraged buyout firm, leaned on a group of friends for $1 million apiece, raising $53 million to start. But, he said to them, "I don't just want the million dollars. I want your people, their expertise, their time."[26] This set the standard for corporate involvement in the Fund's activities and investments. The Fund's network now consists of more than 250 business and finance leaders in New York who are engaged at the level of personal interest in at least one of the Fund's rich portfolio of investments.

Moral Imagination and Market Sensibility

Together with the moral vitality of Halftime and the civic purposefulness of the Newark Alliance, the New York City Investment Fund honestly recognizes the importance of individuals imbued with a sense of community obligation. And the Jobs Partnership, ServiceMaster, Pioneer Human Services, and the Roberts Enterprise Development Fund are all driven by people who not only seek benefits to their business interests but who have a deep concern for the social stability of their communities. In short, a humane economy is not built out of a happy and accidental concurrence of social objectives with market opportunity, but from the moral imagination of individuals with a deep commitment to *both* social stability *and* economic well-being. These individuals have all acted upon an understanding that social health requires economic health, and vice versa.

It should also be noted that the individuals and organizations in each of these examples either operate squarely within, or rely upon, the social sector for the accomplishment of their goals. ServiceMaster partners with homeless shelters.

The Jobs Partnership is a nonprofit matchmaker between churches and businesses. Bob Buford founded a nonprofit organization to promote his Halftime message. The New York City Investment Fund does not only invest in companies but also nonprofits that contribute to the flourishing of the Big Apple. And so it goes. A humane economy has to lean upon the institutions and organizations that can do the humanizing; and these, it turns out, are largely social sector entities.

Conclusion: A New Economy?

Boston College's Severyn Bruyn, a longtime student of the interaction between the social sector and the economy, argues that the influence of civil society's institutions on the health of our market economy is more than window dressing. They provide self-regulation in ways that keep government from doing so, and they help reign in the destructiveness of big business on communities. Throughout the historical development of our market economy, he writes, "the quiet creation of social standards and self-enforcement in [churches, youth organizations, hospitals, colleges, and universities] helped civilize relationships among people who were often in competition or conflict with one another."[27] He terms these types of organizations "civil associations" and calls them "a latent force in the competitive system, evolving, unpublicized, as a part of the matrix of associations in the economy."[28]

The interplay between social and market sectors creates what Bruyn calls a "civil economy," which is similar to what Röpke called a "humane economy." It is the economy understood in terms of the moralizing and humanizing forces of civil associations, or the social sector. It holds together the values and principles essential to our entire political economy. Bruyn writes:

> Theoretically, civil economy develops from democratic associations and civic organizations promoting social capital with the principles of democracy, freedom, and justice as well as profitability, efficiency, and productivity. The problem in cultivating a civil economy is dependent upon whether these different values can be linked effectively. The practice of civil economy articulates this integral process.[29]

Civil associations create a civilizing pressure on the marketplace in numerous ways. Bruyn has identified eleven forms of "inter-sector relations" in which the social sector and the market sector create a balance in which self-regulation of economic activity occurs. These relations range from the conflict resolution made possible outside of the court system by nonprofit professional and trade associations to creative partnerships for taking care of social problems to the inter-sector ownership of social sector funds invested in market institutions. In all cases, inter-sector relations, which include the kinds of examples I have cited in this chapter, between market activity and the social sector create an interplay that allows each to influence and permeate the other's environment.

Yet we understand these relations all too little. Our sectored economy and the hoards of experts who know the inner workings of one sector (but rarely two) combine to persuade us that there is nothing to understand. And yet it is clear that a broader range of concerns and commonly held public values are met when our sectors cooperate. We need to dedicate more research, inquiry, and activity to help us build our understanding of the civil, or humane, economy. "The creative interplay of forces in different sectors," Bruyn writes, "could represent a path toward greater progress, justice, mutuality, and freedom."[30] That, most people should agree, is reason enough to begin building a stronger, more humane economy.

Notes

1. John Hale, *The Civilization of Europe in the Renaissance* (New York: Touchstone, 1993), 374.
2. Gerald O'Driscoll, Kim Holmes, and Mary Anastasia O'Grady, "Repression Breeds Terrorism," *Wall Street Journal*, November 12, 2001, A22.
3. Adam Smith, *The Theory of Moral Sentiments* (Indianapolis: Liberty Fund, 1984), 220, 219-221.
4. Wilhelm Röpke, *A Humane Economy: The Social Framework of the Free Market* (Chicago: Henry Regnery, 1960), 105.
5. Röpke, *A Humane Economy*, 124.
6. Röpke, 125.
7. Röpke, 109.
8. Röpke, 104.
9. Röpke, 104.
10. Röpke, 130.
11. Röpke, 131.
12. Röpke, 149.
13. For an extended case study of the Jobs Partnership, as well as of the Service-Master and Roberts Enterprise Development Fund examples that follow, see my *Transforming Charity: Toward a Results-Oriented Social Sector* (Indianapolis: Hudson Institute, 2001), chapter two.
14. "Pioneer Spirit," *Puget Sound Business Journal* (November 14, 1997).
15. For details on REDF's SROI philosophy and copies of the SROI reports for its portfolio enterprises, see http://www.redf.org/pub_sroi.htm.
16. John J. Havens and Paul G. Schervish, *Millionaires and the Millennium: New Estimates of the Forthcoming Wealth Transfer and the Prospects for a Golden Age of Philanthropy* (Boston: Social Welfare Research Institute, 1999), 1.
17. Cited on Boston College's Social Welfare Research Institute web site, http://www.bc.edu/swri/.
18. Peter Drucker, "The New Demographics" and "The New Society," *The Economist* (November 1, 2001).
19. Bob Buford, *Halftime: Changing Your Game Plan from Success to Significance* (Grand Rapids: Harper Collins/Zondervan, 1994), 20, 30.

20. Peter Drucker, preface to Buford, *Halftime*, 14.

21. Drucker, preface to Buford.

22. "Building on Newark's Renaissance," *Business News New Jersey* (October 16, 2001).

23. Peter Plastrik and Kathryn Wylde, *The New York City Investment Fund: An Emerging Model for Corporate Engagement in Urban Development*, Capital Xchange (Center on Urban and Metropolitan Policy, Brookings Institution & Joint Center for Housing Studies, Harvard University, 2001), 2, 3.

24. Plastrik and Wylde, *The New York City Investment Fund*, 2.

25. Plastrik and Wylde, 9.

26. Plastrik and Wylde, 5.

27. Severyn Bruyn, *A Civil Economy: Transforming the Market in the Twenty-First Century* (Ann Arbor: University of Michigan Press, 2000), 12.

28. Bruyn, *A Civil Economy*, 12.

29. Bruyn, 265-66, note 32.

30. Bruyn, 34.

PART THREE

Moral Habits and the Public Good

Chapter Seven

Families, Fathers, and Citizenship

Don Eberly

Seedbeds of Citizenship

The sociologist David Popenoe argues that the success of every society depends upon its ability to produce a large number of adults who are good citizens and who uphold high standards. The central task of a democracy, therefore, is for older generations to devote themselves to socializing infants into adults, a process which transforms self-interested private individuals into public-spirited citizens. Democracy is heavily dependent for its success upon those institutions which perform that socializing task, especially parents.

What is easily forgotten is that democratic society is fragile. It is like a garden: it takes much care and cultivation. Ben Franklin captured this idea when, as he was leaving the 1787 Constitutional Convention, he said: "We have ourselves a republic, if we can keep it." Preserving democracy requires far more than merely maintaining the machinery of elections, lawmaking, and public administration—the kinds of things that seem to dominate our public conversation.

Far more important is the substantive content of democracy. American democracy requires individuals in large numbers who possess a capacity for self-governance. Democracy, in short, requires democrats.

The Founders mentioned little about the social building blocks of democracy. It appears that they merely assumed that succeeding generations would take pains to cultivate character and maintain strong character-shaping institutions such as families and communities.

Those who wish to restore civil society must concern themselves with the following questions: How do people come by their capacity for self-mastery and citizenship? By what means does the human person proceed from infancy to become a caring, conscientious adult? By what process does the individual acquire democratic habits, skills, and values? How is moral conscience, so vital for a civil and humane society, formed? The short answer to these questions is civil society, and all of the life-enhancing institutions that make it up.

Many Americans are deeply worried that we are doing too poor a job of passing along character to the young. Citizens are puzzled and deeply dismayed that in the midst of extraordinary prosperity and success, some of the worst problems a society could have persist—crime, drugs, teen pregnancy, family fragmentation, and a host of other ills affecting children and youth. They are baffled that prosperity does not necessarily translate into a more decent society.

When a polling firm asked Americans to identify the part of our society where "an effort to do better" would make the biggest difference, the most frequently chosen answer was "strengthening the family."[1]

Little Platoons

Edmund Burke described the organic bonds of membership in the small community of the family as "little platoons." Alexis de Tocqueville said we must be attached to these little "subdivisions" that we belong to in society, which are the "first link" in a series by which we proceed toward a love of our country and of mankind generally. They are the foundation on which "the progress of all the rest depends." In and through these "subdivisions" of society "feelings and opinions are recruited, the heart is enlarged, and the human mind is developed by the reciprocal influence we have on one another."

Is it possible that the maintenance of our democratic regime falls largely to families? Tocqueville certainly seemed to imply that. He observed that the basic democratic prerequisites—the habits of the heart—as he put it, would be nourished and transmitted from generation to generation through the family.

There are real consequences for civil society when these small webs of connection are fractured. It is through these most intimate bonds of human affiliation in the family and kin, where we learn to grow and struggle with people who love us passionately, which then enables us to learn to trust, respect, and even appreciate those with whom we disagree in the wider democratic society. Disagreement and conflict are manageable because we are bound together in some larger whole.

Family is often celebrated as a place of love, warmth, and affection, which of course it is, or at least should be. But it is also an arena of conflict where we are locked into struggle with each other and it is that struggle, not its absence, that causes us to grow. One envisions the picture of concentric circles of trust, starting with the most intimate and durable, and moving out to the less personal and less secure.

The case for the family is well known. We Americans have been talking and arguing about the family for decades now, and it has often been a rather acrimonious debate. In many ways, however, the debate has matured recently as a far wider consensus has begun to take shape. Many changes have come to the family, and certainly not all of them are negative. For example, most people can appreciate the shifting and expansion of roles for both men and women across the spheres of home and workplace.

Fatherlessness

However, one consequence of family change which is decidedly not positive is that fewer and fewer children are being raised by committed, involved fathers. In fact, any reference to family fragmentation must be understood as virtually synonymous with the absence of fathers, since the consequence of family breakup in over 90 percent of the cases is that children are being raised apart from their fathers.

Some will assert that this has always been a problem, which is certainly true to some extent. Societies, including our own, have always had a certain percentage of father absence in various forms. Fathers have always left home for work or war, sometimes for long periods of time, sometimes never returning. Moreover, we have always had a certain amount of divorce and a certain amount of nonmarital births. And in all too many cases, dating back to the beginning of recorded human history, there have been fathers who have been largely dysfunctional—perhaps physically present, but in all other respects disengaged. The family has always been under stress to some degree and always will be.

But what American society is now having to cope with is radically different, in both its scale and its nature. Whereas father absence has always been a challenge, it was once the exception to the rule, whereas today it is on its way to becoming the rule, and this is not good for children.

University of Chicago professor Don Browning, who is one of the nation's leading family scholars, writes: "Father absence is an unprecedented reality in our society. It is not a manufactured issue. The problem of vast numbers of children being raised without resident fathers has not been fabricated by political conservatives, alarmist social scientists, or the media." "Furthermore," he writes, "the phenomenon is unprecedented; it has never happened in this fashion and to this degree before."[2]

By fashion and degree, Browning means that there is voluntary father absence, not separation due to death, and it is occurring on a large, unprecedented scale. The number of children living only with their mothers in 1960 was 5.1 million. Today, the number of children going to bed in a household in which the biological father does not live is pushing 24 million, or almost 40 percent of all children. Thirty-two percent of the children born today are to nonmarried, father-absent households, and one in every two will spend a portion of his or her lifetime apart from their fathers.[3]

Space does not permit an entire review of how this has come to pass. There was a time not long ago when many concluded that fathers did not make a unique, gender-specific contribution to the nurturance of children, implying that any number of possible substitutes would be fine. In recent decades, many have entertained the idea that children were more resilient in cases of family breakup than they actually are, which almost always has meant far less time with the father. Many influences, both cultural and economic, contributed to the change.

Social outcomes have multiple explanations, especially in a society as complex as ours. Nevertheless, the proposition that attracts almost no opposition from policy and social science experts today is that family fragmentation and fatherlessness are leading contributors to many forms of maladjustment among children.

Over the past decade, a voluminous body of data has documented the ill effects of growing up without a father. Fatherless children, for example, are five times more likely to live in poverty, three times more likely to fail in school, two or three times more likely to experience emotional or behavioral problems, and three times more likely to commit suicide.

What research does not suggest, and what is not being suggested here, is that children who are raised in single-parent households are bound by some immutable law to fail in school, turn to drugs, or commit crime. Kids from father-absent households can and do become merit scholars, all-star athletes, and professional successes, and even for those who don't excel, many grow up to be fine citizens. Good single mothers and good nonresidential fathers can make a major difference.

That said, however, neither can we deny the basic evidence confirming that a host of negative outcomes for kids are strongly tied to the presence or absence of fathers. According to Urie Bronfenbrenner, controlling for factors such as low income, children growing up in father-absent households are at greater risk for experiencing a variety of behavioral and educational problems, including extremes of hyperactivity and withdrawal; lack of attentiveness in the classroom; difficulty in deferring gratification; impaired academic achievement; social misbehavior; absenteeism; dropping out; involvement in socially alienated peer groups; and the so-called 'teen-age syndrome' of behaviors that tend to hang together—smoking, drinking, vandalism, violence, and criminal acts.[4]

Social Consequences

Perhaps no factor is more powerful or disturbing than the undeniable tie of father absence to poverty. A father-absent society is a society in which growing numbers of children are poor. Poverty has many root causes, but none so decisive or powerful as father absence. According to the National Commission on Children, almost 75 percent of America's children who live in single-parent families will experience poverty before turning eleven years of age, whereas the majority of kids from father-present families will never experience poverty. Child poverty rates would be one-third to one-half lower today if family structure had not changed so dramatically since 1960.[5]

Equally troubling is the contribution fatherlessness makes to antisocial activity. American society is paying a huge price for having failed to heed the warning issued by Daniel Patrick Moynihan in 1965, when he stated that "a community that allows a large number of young men to grow up in broken homes, dominated by women, never acquiring any stable relationship to male authority, never acquiring any expectation about the future—that community asks for and gets chaos."[6]

Males acting out against the social order is widespread and comes in numerous forms, from behavior that is merely obnoxious to that which is socially menacing. Evidence of its impact can be found in every sector of American society, and not just from the perpetrators of violence in our cities and small towns. It includes not merely the poor, but many from the upper strata of society, such as world-famous athletes and entertainment celebrities.

Consider the case of Howard Stern, the "shock jock" radio host who looks for new ways to titillate and offend each day, usually through degrading sexual references to women. Stern talked about his father recently in an interview with *Rolling Stone* magazine. Says Stern: "The way I was raised, my father was always telling me I was a piece of (expletive). I think I'll go to my grave not feeling very positive about myself or that I'm very, very special."[7]

Or consider the case of Dennis Rodman, the profane and outrageous basketball player. Rodman attributes his often perverse performance as a sports celebrity to the example of his father, who has fathered twenty-seven children to numerous women, while otherwise largely ignoring his offspring.[8]

Bill Stephney, who runs an entertainment company in New York and tracks trends and issues within the music industry, reports that the vast majority of gang members and violent rappers live out their lives of rage because of missing fathers. In fact, he reports that the theme of anger toward the father who was never there is emerging as a major new trend in rap music. In a rap song "Father," LL Cool J sings "all I ever wanted, all I ever needed, was a father."[9]

The most socially destructive form of aggressive acting out which is tied powerfully back to father absence is crime. Seventy-two percent of adolescents serving sentences for murder are from fatherless households. Sixty percent of the rapists and over 70 percent of the long-term correctional facility inmates are from father-absent households.[10]

Few things are more threatening to civil society than crime and violence. Recent studies indicate that the chief predictor of crime in a neighborhood is not poverty or race, but the proportion of households in which fathers are missing. When you take the presence or absence of fathers into account, the relationship of crime to income as well as race disappears.[11]

Noted social scientist James Q. Wilson has said that "every society must be wary of the unattached male, for he is universally the cause of numerous social ills. The good society is heavily dependent on men being attached to a strong moral order centered on families, both to discipline their sexual behavior and to reduce their competitive aggression."[12]

Curbing the aggressive impulses of young males is perhaps the greatest challenge that falls to fathers. As the national news regularly reports, today in American society there is an unusually large number of young people who seem to be very, very angry, who appear wound up like a tightly coiled spring, waiting to explode at the slightest provocation.

The nation has been served a stream of shocking reports of brutal schoolyard shootings by young males. In defiance of stereotypes, all of the shootings have occurred in small, rural communities, by young white males from average, middle-class backgrounds. Shawn Johnson, a California-based forensic psychologist who has conducted over 6,000 evaluations of adult and juvenile criminals states: "this is the price we are paying as a society for the number of fathers who have bailed out on their children."[13]

Obviously, only a small minority of troubled kids will turn to slaughtering others in cold blood, and certainly father absence is not the only factor behind this growing epidemic. Nevertheless, the alienation among youth and even young children today is widespread.

Children—both boys and girls—need to see examples of confident males turning their energies toward affirming life and nourishing character, not the pseudo-masculinity of power or domination. Those who have studied masculinity have remarked about its basic fragility. It is all too easy for masculinity, which is held together tenuously by societal norms, to fall out of kilter when too few fathers are there to model it out in all of its complexities of strength and tenderness, initiative, and restraint. When these supports are not in place, society suffers, not from too much genuine masculinity, but from far too little of it.

Mending the Male

A society of too few mature fathers ends up with what Dr. Frank Pittman calls "toxic masculinity," where essentially weak, insecure, and poorly fathered men chase after a socially destructive masculine mystique. Men who have not fully felt the love and approval of their fathers are men who live in masculine shame. Says Pittman, "men without models don't know what is behind their shame, loneliness, and despair, their desperate search for love, for affirmation and for structure, their frantic tendency to compete over just about anything with just about anybody." These men are in a battle not with women, whether their mothers, wives, or girlfriends, as much as with their own fathers.[14]

Says Pittman, boys who want to become men have to "guess at what men are like" which usually turns out being what he calls a "pathologically exaggerated masculinity." Whatever the challenge, these men are never "man enough." What is the way out of this trap of shrunken, shame-filled masculinity? "Ultimately," says Pittman, "we're not going to raise a better class of men until we have a better class of fathers." The answer, he says, is the forgotten profession of fatherhood.[15]

The tendency in focusing on what one expert termed "the male problematic" is to neglect the consequences of father absence in the lives of girls and young women. Poorly fathered girls often fall victim to poorly fathered young men who prey on the vulnerabilities of girls who carry within them a hunger for the father's affection and who confuse it with false and costly alternatives. Girls from father-absent households are 164 percent more likely to have children out of wedlock, often starting in their teens.

Fathers and Socialization

It is not enough to describe the consequences of father absence without detailing the positive contributions fathers make in nurturing children. What relevance, we might ask, does fatherhood have to the cultivation of those positive ingredients of citizenship such as trust, cooperation, and social generosity among citizens?

To what extent, in other words, is the restoration of father-involved families integral to the renewal of American civil society? The family benefits society by producing what scholars call social capital. James Coleman, who popularized the term "social capital," utilized the phrase to describe a range of personal strengths that are cultivated in the family, especially the ability to form ties of cooperation and to work toward common purposes.

Social capital refers to personal capacities such as the important civic capacity to be helpful, trustful, and respectful in relationship to one's associates and is clearly affected by patterns of trust and interdependency learned in families. Deficits in social capital created in our families quickly come to affect the social health of the nation.

Trust

Consider the issue of trust, perhaps the most vital ingredient of democratic society. Much has been made of the fact that large majorities of the American people are distrustful of their public institutions. Now we have discovered the unsurprising fact that American citizens are more and more distrustful and suspicious of each other. Fewer than half of Americans report being able to trust "most of the people most of the time." Contrary to convenient myth, our discontents are not confined to governmental malfeasance and feckless politicians. A more likely source of our cynicism is the rupture of our primary relationships within the family, of our marriages and homes, and especially of the connection of children to fathers.

Trust is nurtured in the family. In bonding to the children, the parent puts in place the rudiments of trust: a process which, according to family scholar Urie Bronfenbrenner, conveys "a strong, mutual, irrational, emotional attachment" offered through a person who "is committed to the child's well-being and development, preferably for life." Much like economic capital, social capital can be drawn down.

Who can doubt that a child will be less trusting or cooperative as an adult if he or she has experienced a painful loss of trust in the person in whom he thought he could surely place his trust, his own father? Disillusionment with our primary relationships leads to distrust of kin and community.

Youth Alienation

Or consider the phenomenon of youth alienation. The George Gallup organization conducts an annual Youth Survey to reflect what is happening with "real teens" as a group. Wondering why so many American teens are depressed or alienated, the Gallup Youth Survey proceeded to search for answers to this question by constructing an "alienation index." Gallup concluded that a deprived family life seems to be the key "cause" indicator of alienation. Often there is simply a huge disconnect between the lives of parents—little to talk about, little in common, extreme busyness. In many cases, one of the parents, most frequently the father, is simply not there for them.

Never before have so many children been so far removed from the things that give life a sense of direction, meaning, and purpose: one's heritage, place, and people. In no case is this alienation deeper than in the fraying of family bonds, and the separation of children from their fathers.

As inherently social and meaning-seeking creatures, human beings possess a need for membership in human community—for connection, cohesion, and coherence. When these needs are not met, individuals experience painful isolation and society suffers. Our's is an anonymous, fast-paced, and increasingly impersonal society, but a leading cause of uprootedness among the young is not these factors, but rather the declining reliability of a growing number of parents to preserve the bonds of affection and trust with their own children.

If adults in the home are caring, fair, and faithful under all circumstances, then that is what the child will likely expect from, and be capable of displaying in, the world beyond the home. Conversely, if the experience the child had of home was one of abuse, neglect, or betrayal, it is not surprising that they project attitudes of cynicism and hopelessness toward the broader society. It is hard to imagine attitudes of general trust taking shape toward more remote political and social institutions when a child is abandoned or betrayed by a mother or father.

Authority

Or consider the example of authority. Parents are the first encounter kids have with authority. How interaction with that intimate form of authority takes shape will likely determine the child's success at navigating his or her way through the more challenging territory of authority and conflict in the school, on the playground, or at the mall. In many ways, healthy fathers serve as a bridge between the more protected life of the home and the more demanding environment of the world beyond. Fathers raise their children mostly with an eye toward their inevitable encounter with the rules and norms of the world beyond the nest. Good fathers tutor their children toward developing positive habits of self-control and respect toward others.

A final core ingredient of civil society supplied by families, especially fathers, is impulse control. This is one of the most important functions that fathers carry out in the socialization of children, especially young males. Wade Horn, prominent child psychologist and president of the National Fatherhood Initiative, points out that proper socialization requires the development of the ability to delay or inhibit impulse gratification. According to Horn, "well-socialized children have learned not to strike out at others to get what they want; undersocialized children have not. Well-socialized children have learned to listen to and obey the directions of legitimate authority figures, such as parents and teachers; undersocialized children have not." He notes that studies which demonstrate the differences between the way fathers and mothers parent indicate that fathers are essential to helping the young develop impulse control, and to be socially cooperative.

Renewing Fatherhood as a Social Norm

If the renewal of father-involved families is central to the restoration of civil society, we cannot afford to be agnostic on several related questions that concern not just whether fathering takes place, but how and under what circumstances it is likely to be carried out.

It is nearly impossible to discuss the renewal of fatherhood in isolation from other social and cultural realities that are now common in America. For example, the vagueness of our recent discussion of family reflects our need to accommodate a steep rise in separated, divorced, blending, and never-formed families headed in the vast majority of cases by single mothers. To some, family now means little more than a collection of adults bound together by temporary needs and agreements. This relativization of the family also fits comfortably with the broadly felt desire among adults to embrace the dramatic expansion of private lifestyle choices. This exaltation of private adult choice has not served the needs of children well.

It is important that a discussion of fatherhood be addressed to all fathers. Even though many fathers are removed from the households in which their children are being raised, we must acknowledge their desire in many cases to care for their offspring, and the importance of such care, even under circumstances that are extremely difficult. This is important, especially in urban America where nonmarital births are the large majority and where fathers, if they are engaged at all, are involved through arrangements with the mothers of their children.

Having presented this, however, it is necessary to point out that embracing an elastic notion of family out of a legitimate desire to improve fathering may have the unintended consequence of making the job harder to accomplish in the future. That engaged fathering is hard to maintain apart from the intact family is borne out by research indicating that approximately 40 percent of the children who live in fatherless households have not seen their fathers in the past year and of the remaining 60 percent, only 20 percent spend one night per month in the father's home.[16]

To put the problem plainly, the immediate consequence of this relativization of the definition of the family is that fathers are the first to be written out of the family script. When the cutting and pasting begins on the ever-changing family portrait, it is the father who is typically cut out. In the vast majority of cases, children from fragmented families live apart from their fathers and in many cases see him infrequently.

Reasserting a basic family norm of two parents, preferably the biological parents, preferably parenting cooperatively in the context of marriage, depends largely on the validity of the claim that fathers are essential in the contribution they make. Historically, societies have not had to worry that mothers might fall short of fulfilling their biologically determined role; voluntary mother-absence has not occurred broadly across time and human societies. This is obviously not true with fathers.

Fathering, says family sociologist John Miller, is "a cultural acquisition to an extent that mothering is not." Given the fact that there are few biologically compelling reasons for the male to care for his offspring, "a set of overlapping largely cultural developments" are required. When a culture "ceases to support a father's involvement with his own children (through its law, mores, symbols, models, rituals) powerful natural forces take over in favor of the mother only family."[17]

Conclusion

Democratic character flows not from formal constitutions or congressional acts, but from vital, character-shaping institutions in society, of which the family is the most foundational. According to Harvard University professor Mary Ann Glendon, "Governments must have an adequate supply of citizens who are skilled in the arts of self-government." According to Glendon, these arts consist of "deliberation, compromise, consensus-building, civility, and reason-giving."

The decline in fathering and father absence (whether through the growing prevalence of physical absence of some or merely emotional disengagement by others) contribute to socially underdeveloped citizens who often lack the necessary disposition for healthy participation in society. Fathers can be powerfully positive factors in making better citizens.

In sum, liberal democratic values flower when rooted in the subsoil of vibrant institutions. Periodically in American history, citizens have reacted to the general disregard of social standards and obligations and, with the help of society-wide social reform movements, moved individuals toward restraint and social obligation. In the nineteenth century, for example, society witnessed an explosion of voluntary associations and organizations aimed at social reform and moral uplift. Spiritual awakenings, temperance movements, and many private and public efforts were made to strengthen character and responsibility. These were dynamic movements that transcended politics and partisanship.

James Q. Wilson, who has tracked social reforms, says that "throughout history, the institutions that have produced effective male socialization have been private, not public." If this is true, he says, "then our policy ought to identify, evaluate and encourage those local, private efforts that seem to do the best job at reducing drug abuse, inducing people to marry, persuading parents, especially fathers, to take responsibility for their children, and exercising informal social controls over neighborhood streets."[18]

The renewal of father-involved families and the renewal of civil society go hand in hand. Fathers have much to offer in socializing children into responsible citizens and will play a key role in strengthening America's communities. Conversely, community-based institutions must be mobilized to strengthen fathers—to reinforce their importance, to offer training and assistance, and to help them pass on to their children a strong fathering heritage.

Notes

1. Peter D. Hart and Robert Teeter, *Wall Street Journal/NBC News Poll*, December 5-8, 1996, 24.

2. Don Eberly, "Fatherhood, the Academy, and the Liberal Churches." In *The Faith Factor in Fatherhood*, ed. Don Eberly (Lanham, Md.: Lexington, 1999).

3. Wade F. Horn, *Father Facts* (Gaithersburg, Md.: National Fatherhood Initiative, 1996), 1.

4. Urie Bronfenbrenner, "Discovering What Families Do." In *Rebuilding the Nest: A New Commitment to the American Family*, ed. David Blankenhorn, S. Bayne, and J.B. Elshtain (Milwaukee: Manticore, 1991), 29.

5. Horn, *Father Facts*, 37.

6. David Broder, "Beware of the Unattached Male," *Washington Post*, February 16, 1994.

7. Interview with Howard Stern, *Rolling Stone*, February 10, 1994, 28-53.

8. Perspectives, *Newsweek*, September 9, 1996, 25.

9. Veronica Chambers, "Family Rappers," *Newsweek*, January 19, 1998, 42.

10. Horn, *Father Facts*, 32-33.

11. Horn, *Father Facts*, 32.

12. Broder, "Beware of the Unattached Male."

13. Elizabeth Kastor, "When Kids Kill," *Washington Post*, in *Lancaster Sunday News*, Lancaster, Pa., April 5, 1996, 1.

14. Frank Pittman, *Man Enough: Fathers, Sons and the Search for Masculinity* (New York: Berkley, 1993), xx.

15. Pittman, *Man Enough*, xxi.

16. Horn, *Father Facts*, 1.

17. John Miller, *Biblical Faith and Fathering: Why We Call God Father* (New York: Paulist Press, 1989), 2.

18. James Q. Wilson, "Culture, Incentives, and the Underclass." In *Values and Public Policy* (Washington, D.C.: Brookings, 1994), 74.

Chapter Eight

Cultivating Moral Habits
Four Social Virtues Worth the Work

Ryan Streeter

This point of this chapter is simple: our moral condition is improved not merely by improving our ethics (getting the rules right) but by cultivating moral habits (getting our lives right). The former without the latter gives us a society bent on legalities and procedures without the manners and public sensibility needed for a robust, healthy democracy. The cultivation of moral habits requires the right kinds of social contexts in which habits can be taught and reinforced—families, neighborhoods, schools, local social networks, religious institutions, and work teams. Good ethics, on the other hand, can be learned by reading a book or going to a seminar.

A person can be ethical without being moral, but a moral person is always ethical (except in rare cases where socially accepted ethical rules are unjust) and more. Being ethical is being true to the rules that are on the books, or at most, being true to the spirit of the rules. Being moral requires the exercise of habits that make sure we apply rules in their best light and do the right thing even in the absence of rules.

People preoccupied with being ethical are usually concerned about being right. People preoccupied with being moral are usually concerned about being good. Whereas ethics places our focus on the rules that govern behavior, moral living places our focus on the kind of person each of us is. It goes without saying that being moral is a greater challenge than being ethical.

As a term, "morality" suffers from an ignominy that "ethics" escapes. It is fashionable to be known for being ethical, while being known as moral is liable to raise eyebrows—being moral is often equated with being prudish. However, a society marked by a preoccupation with ethics instead of morality suffers from the preoccupation with legalism that most Americans complain about.

In societies preoccupied with morality, every citizen has a priest. In societies preoccupied with ethics, every citizen has a lawyer. In the former, a young couple considering marriage consults their priest, who asks them to make sacrifices so that their marriage works. In the latter, the couple visits their attorney, who asks them for their signatures on a prenuptial agreement, which determines in advance what they will do once each has grown weary of the other's unwillingness to make sacrifices.

Americans are have undoubtedly grown more legalistic—an odd proposition in the wake of the 1960s mentality that prides itself on breaking the rules and just being "true to yourself." And while most Americans would not want to return to the kind of authoritarian moralities of the past idealized by the right and demonized by the left, less reliance on lawsuits and legal nitpicking—and more reliance on the good sense of strong families and communities—would come as a welcome change to many. Lawsuits are on the rise in everything from the construction industry to the hospital sector to even the educational arena. Human resources managers are buying Employment Practices Liability Insurance, and the Equal Employment Opportunity Commission reports a 30.1 percent rise between 1992 and 2000 in "no reasonable cause" cases—or, cases in which the evidence suggests that no discrimination has occurred. These cases represent 68.3 percent of all cases filed with the commission.[1]

The American preoccupation with legalism and ethics signifies a deeper problem than more lawsuits and mounting ethics oversight costs. It signifies a loss of moral substance. By moral substance, I mean the ability to cultivate the affections, dispositions, and behaviors on which our kind of society—the democratic republican kind—depends. Democratic republics depend upon people who make sacrifices at the same time they are aggressively pursuing their objectives, who aim for what is noble while extending grace to those who act ignobly, and who are fair in their dealings even while suspecting that others—and especially those with a lot of power—are prone to unfairness.

Bumper Sticker Morality

Unfortunately, our legalistic society tends toward the other end of the scale. We try to force others to make sacrifices on our behalf. We relish the ignoble and pretend that "noble" is a fiction. We maintain a pretense of suspicion for our elites in general while worshiping celebrities and expecting political powerbrokers to attend to our ever more mundane concerns.

But these problems do not even get to the heart of the matter. The real problem is that we have grown too comfortable with bumper sticker morality. Bumper sticker morality concerns itself with grand principles and "commitments." It thinks globally and stumbles locally. It is beholden to ideology but devoid of principled practice. It lets others know "where you stand" without saying a thing about who you are. It is morality for the highway, where people move at lightning speed, rushing to the next thing, unable to see each other's faces. Bumper sticker morality comes in two general types. The first is regrettable but relatively harmless to society as a whole, but the second, depending on its degree of intensity, can be quite harmful.

Cheap Commitment

This is the first type of bumper sticker morality. It is the moral predicament of the anticapitalist who proselytizes his fellow graduate students with his Marxist platitudes while sipping a venti vanilla latte at Starbucks, which he paid for with money from his trust fund. It is the morality of the pro-life activist who is harsh with his own children and mean to his neighbors' kids. It is the firm stance of the "I-hate-the-sin-not-the-sinner" churchgoer who hates his next door neighbors for letting the dogs bark too long before calling them in. It is the conviction of the leftist moral libertarian ("do what's right for you!") who complains that his colleagues holding a Bible study during prework hours are infringing on his rights, though he cannot articulate exactly which rights.

Cheap commitments come easily, but acting morally at home, with consistency, requires effort—or moral habits. Cheap commitment is the secular version of Dietrich Bonhöffer's "cheap grace." Bonhöffer had no patience for self-proclaimed Christians who accept divine grace without feeling compelled to do anything in return.[2] Cheap commitment, likewise, provides a sense of moral importance but demands little action from the "believer." It is easy to seek acceptance in a group by reciting its creeds. It is quite another to live the creeds.

Those who live by cheap commitments suffer from a fundamental disjunction between the creeds they defend and the creeds they actually practice every day. The cheaply committed rolls into his driveway, his bumpers plastered with slogans, while his neighbors, who have to put up with his daily lack of neighborliness, roll their eyes in disbelief that someone so "morally committed" could be so morally disabled. The cheaply committed feels emboldened by believing in certain principles, ethics, and creeds. He is much less inspired to actually live them out.

In the end, the cheaply committed is a failure by his own standards, but he is saved by the creed of the neighborhood, the workplace, the faith community. His most sensible morality is that which he lives every day in spite of his beliefs. He sacrifices his leisure time to rake the leaves because everyone else on his street does so. He works hard because his boss expects it. He kneels to pray because his soul, he acknowledges, requires humility. His private life contains within it the principles of a sound public morality, while his public commitments are extreme and make him a fool in the eyes of those who know him privately. If only he would preach what he already believes.

Narrow Commitment

This is the second kind of bumper sticker morality, and it is more dangerous than the first. Cheap commitment might hurt the cheaply committed in the long run, but it does little harm to others. Narrow commitment, on the other hand, makes the mistake of trying to cram a complex and large world into a box too simple and small to contain it. The narrowly committed expect reality to conform itself to their overly simplified ideas about what is right—and they grow frustrated when reality does not cooperate.

Narrow commitment is an incomplete moral stance. It is a moral framework that explains away complex sets of problems with one or two simple principles that, in reality, are unable to deal with complexity. It is usually a philosophical problem at heart in which the culprit takes some rule of thumb or a belief that is true in some cases and then universalizes it to all cases. Narrow commitment lacks the courage to look real-life problems in the eye and deal with all their aspects.

This is the moral framework of the activist who believes that all social inequities are the result of capitalism, or the libertarian who believes that the federal government is solely responsible for all imaginable social ills, or the education reformer who explains poor student performance as the result of inadequate funding for buildings and teachers alone, or the right-wing fundamentalist who blames the removal of prayer from schools for all our educational woes. The postmodern misanthrope who judges someone's merit only on the basis of race, class, and sexual orientation—and overlooks faith or vocational path or community service—falls into this camp. So do religious fundamentalists who view the world far more extremely than their religious texts or traditions do.

In each case, the narrowly committed person takes a legitimate concern or approximate belief, which has independent merit, and then tries to apply it to everything in his or her path. It is right to be concerned about corporations who put profit before people, but that does not make all corporate activity unjust. That government programs have created perverse dependencies among distressed populations does not make all government programming suspect. Proponents of extreme political views flatly ignore the good produced by what they criticize, such as the spread of liberty, widespread increases in standards of living, better health and so on.

The narrowly committed suffer from what Jean Bethke Elshtain has called "totalism." Elshtain describes totalism as the belief that solutions to social problems can be achieved in a "total restructuring of society" according to a few strict ideological principles. In reality, she points out, this would require massive oversight and extensive policing (which totalists denounce in other contexts) because making the world fit into narrow categories requires a lot of control. "It is unclear," Elshtain writes, "whether such a society would be democratic or whether, indeed, there would be any politics worthy of the name at all."[3] Totalist thought disrupts real lives and communities by pursuing ideological aims that are disconnected from any life or community.

It is difficult to deny that we live in an age of ideology—if by ideology we understand cheap and narrow commitment. Ideological devotion finds expression in commitment to abstract ideas that are difficult to put into practice. But people try. And this results in bad, even corrupt, policy. Sometimes, policies are simply ludicrous, such as hyper-legalistic dating codes that have recently emerged at some colleges as a result of exaggerated views of male sexual motivation. But sometimes they are destructive, such as the widespread killing that results from commitments to abstract ideals, whether in their secular variety, such as the French revolutionaries' view of liberty, or in their religious form, such as the view of holiness held by some radical Islamic fundamentalists.

A Problem of Principle

A moral framework rooted in ideology is different from one rooted in sound principles. Sound principles are general and guide judgment in particular matters. They are broad enough to allow for flexibility in their application. Ideological views are usually particular perspectives that get universalized and are inflexibly applied.

For example, the principle of human fallibility, especially in its religious expressions, says that all of us have a tendency to make matters worse rather than better because we will sacrifice the good of others for our own interests. This principle has led to the institution of checks and balances in government, to neighborhood forums in which politicians are asked to account for their actions, and to numerous other ways of keeping power and appetite in check. It is, however, radically different from the view, say, that all wealthy or powerful people are corrupt because some wealthy and powerful people have been corrupt, or that all poor people have little desire to be self-sufficient because some poor people have avoided work and preferred welfare. The former principle—that of human fallibility—helps liberal democracy because it applies to everyone and is broad enough to allow for discretion in judgment. The latter ideological views help little.

Bumper sticker morality is prescription without content. Content is supplied by social contexts. Most of the social environments in which we all live every day inherently presuppose moral principles that are important to democracy. Raising children, borrowing lawn equipment from neighbors, going to church, preparing for a presentation in the board room, coaching Little League, going out for drinks with friends—all of these activities contain within them codes of conduct that matter for public life.

Yale's Stephen Carter captures this point well when he colorfully describes a scenario where real-life community norms trump an abstract understanding of something as important as rights:

> Suppose that I purchase a house in a neighborhood where the very friendly people all loan each other tools and where everybody keeps beautiful gardens and neatly trimmed lawns. If I let my grass grow wild and allow the weeds to run rampant in my garden, I am not living up to the expectations of my neighbors . . . . To say that I have a "right" to keep my garden as I like is only a distraction: if such a right exists, what my neighbors believe is that I should not exercise it. If I insist on exercising it anyway, I am demonstrating that I am not interested in membership under the community's rules. So I can hardly complain when one of them refuses to loan me a snow-blower.[4]

An unworkable moral abstraction such as an impracticable "right" falls at the feet of workable everyday morality. We may be able to take our totalist thought and turn it into law at the statehouse or doctrine within the university, but it is much harder to be an ideological zealot in our neighborhoods. Our children, spouses, neighbors, and colleagues require a moral realism from us that we can more easily dispense with in the statehouse or university.

Pursuing societal aims on the basis of abstract, or bumper sticker, morality is a peculiarly modern ailment. David Hume, perhaps the most widely read and discussed British Enlightenment writer in the 1700s, noted that political parties rooted in "abstract speculative principle are known only to modern times, and are perhaps the most extraordinary and unaccountable phenomenon that has yet appeared in human affairs."[5] In earlier times, people fought over interests rooted in fairly concrete things like land or familial rights. Even when kings tried to wage large wars for grander causes, they faced the very practical problem of not being able to persuade landholders to give up their peasants as fighters. In modern times, people began fighting over abstractions. Even the bloody religious wars of Europe were owing to the fact that "philosophy was widely spread over the world"—in other words, these wars were more about abstract principles than viable religious faith.[6] The same could be said for the murderous violence of religious extremists in our world.

The antidote for extreme action based on abstract principles is to cultivate a healthy concern for others, for the community, and for the social order of which one is a part—or what Hume and his contemporaries called "the public." This keeps problems in context and preserves morality as a social, rather than intellectual, endeavor. He writes, "For my part, I shall always be more fond of promoting moderation than zeal; though perhaps the surest way of producing moderation...is to increase our zeal for the public."[7] He calls concern for others "the most material part of virtue"—that is, the most substantive and important part—because a healthy zeal for the public is anchored in it. And zeal for the public minimizes ideological commitments by preoccupying us with the real needs and concerns around us.

This is quite a different view from that advanced by other modern thinkers such as Kant, who believed in the power of reason to identify moral principles in the abstract and then build society's institutions upon them. It is the job of lawmakers, Kant said, to make laws "conform to natural right, which stands in our eyes as a model presented by an idea of reason."[8] Kant believed that reason's identification of a moral principle was enough to obligate us to act accordingly.

Hume, on the other hand, believed that we will only be as obligated as our desire to do so is strong. Without a "zeal for the public," it becomes too easy to ignore our moral obligations or, worse yet, begin forcing them on situations where they do not fit. And we can only develop a zeal for the public by belonging to associations and social environments that get us in the habit of looking out for the needs of others. Otherwise, the best of laws crafted by a calculating reason can become the objects of ideological frenzy. For example, "liberty" without a social environment that provides a balance of authority, good examples, and fairness is a recipe for recklessness. Good principles without good associations are still just ideas—and they are capable of abusive manipulation.

The difference between these two perspectives, exemplified here by Hume and Kant, is more than academic. It is, rather, quite consequential. Gertrude Himmelfarb has incisively shown that the British Enlightenment employed compassion as a weapon against poverty, while the French Enlightenment relied upon reason. Eighteenth-century England was marked by a tripartite effort to improve the condition of the poor: a system of public benevolence based on a sympathetic view of the poor as community fellows who should be helped, a religious gospel of good works toward others, and a political economy aimed at raising the wages and working conditions of the laboring poor. The chief public intellectuals of the day—Francis Hutcheson, the Earl of Shaftesbury, Hume, Adam Smith, Adam Ferguson, and others—argued that reason does little by itself to motivate us to act kindly to those in need. Rather, compassion, which means "feeling with," prompts action on behalf of others.

This philosophical framework led to a flowering of social innovation. Reformers founded societies "for the abolition of the slave trade, and for the care of deserted infants, sick and maimed seamen, orphans of clergymen, prostitutes, the deaf, dumb, and blind. And there were abundant proposals for reform: of the legal system, the poor law, hospitals, prisons, and workhouses."[9] A "Sunday School movement" began that served as "a central feature of working-class community life" as well as a center of learning and religious instruction. "Friendly societies" were launched to provide the poor with insurance for times of need, and England "was the first country (and for a long time the only one) to have a public, secular, national (although locally administered) system of poor relief."[10]

The French Enlightenment, on the other hand, regarded the poor as a class, a group of people different not only in station but practically in kind from their elite fellow citizens. Worse, the French cultural and political leaders regarded them as uneducable. However, they believed it was possible, through reason, to improve the condition of people altogether by freeing them from oppressive social environments. "Where the British idea of compassion lent itself to a variety of practical, meliorative policies to relieve social problems, the French appeal to reason could be satisfied with nothing less than the 'regeneration' of man."[11] However, the practical outworking of "an abstract, elevated reason" was the denigration of "the practical reason of ordinary people" through policies that ended up shredding social bonds and replacing them with fear and disorder.[12]

The problem with morality rooted in reason alone is that it remains an idea to be converted into laws and codes of ethics without doing anything to cultivate peoples' affection for doing what is good. In order to recover the practical and habitual moral frameworks that energize community responsiveness, as was the case in the British Enlightenment, we need to first recover forms of social interaction that equip us with what C. S. Lewis might have called a "morality of the chest."

Lewis wrote that "the head rules the belly though the chest—the seat . . . of Magnanimity—Sentiment—these are the indispensable liaison officers between

cerebral man and visceral man. It may even be said that it is by this middle element that man is man: for by his intellect he is mere spirit and by his appetite
mere animal."[13] Criticizing the authors of a contemporary high school textbook,
who had reduced all moral values to mental projections onto a valueless world,
he wrote, "It is not excess of thought but defect of fertile and generous emotion
that marks [the authors] out. Their heads are no bigger than the ordinary: it is the
atrophy of the chest beneath that makes them seem so."[14]

Our challenge today is to combat the life of the head with the wisdom of the
chest, the realm of empty wishes with earthly action. The challenge today is to
take the abstractions of ethics and root them in the concrete moral habits that
transform us from cheaply and narrowly committed moralists into effective,
active, and contributing members of society.

Otherwise, we may suffer from a moral atrophy that threatens our public life.
Noting the political consequences of moral flabbiness, E. J. Dionne writes, "For
most of us, politics is increasingly abstract, a spectator sport barely worth watch-
ing . . . . True, we still praise democracy incessantly and recommend democracy
to the world. But at home, we do little to promote the virtues that self-
government requires or encourage citizens to believe that public engagement is
worth the time. Our system has become one long-running advertisement against
self-government."[15]

What, then, are the virtues, the habits, of a successful democracy?

Four Social Virtues Worth the Work

There are four social virtues that are critical to the health of American society. They are presupposed by civil society and our most important political institutions. In other words, regardless of how good each of us is at practicing them,
we praise or criticize the behavior of others on the basis of how present or absent these virtues are. The virtues are benevolence, justice, restraint, and entrepreneurship.

Each of these virtues, like all virtues, combines sentiment and action. A virtuous person has trained his or her sentiments to favor doing what is good. He or
she also does good. Someone who only feels like doing good but does not is
weak-willed, what Aristotle called an *akratic* individual—a person who, despite
having good intentions and knowing the best course of action, does not act virtuously. *Akratic* people, in fact, are more troubling than people who simply sur-
render themselves to their passions and do not think about the moral consequences; the latter can be helped, but the former already know what virtue is but
fail to live it out. The *akratic* individual, Aristotle says, "illustrates [an ancient]
proverb, 'If water chokes us, what must we drink to wash it down?'"[16]

Likewise, someone who merely "toes the line" and complies with ethical
standards but does not have the right sentiments is not truly virtuous: this person
cannot be trusted to be virtuous in the absence of rules because the heart is not
trained to seek out and do what is good. To be virtuous is to practice the moral-

ity of the chest. It is to be possessed of sentiments bent on preserving what is good in one's community and improving what is not.

Benevolence, justice, restraint, and entrepreneurship have long supported modern liberal democracy. David Hume and Adam Smith regarded benevolence and justice as the primary social virtues, the bedrock of any healthy civil society. Early Americans from John Witherspoon to Thomas Jefferson to Benjamin Franklin to John Adams to James Madison were familiar with, and advocates for, the primary importance of these virtues.

They understood what we sometimes forget: benevolence and justice must be found at the community level before they can become qualities of the larger society. Without the generosity, goodwill, compassion and neighborliness—in short, benevolence—of everyday citizens, our institutions of public welfare would have a much bigger job to do. And without justice-promoting habits such as fairness and trustworthiness at home, our policing and legal systems would be larger and more intrusive. In other words, without benevolence at the community level, our liberal democracy would be less liberal, and without justice at home, less democratic.

Restraint, sometimes known as self-control, has roots in the Greek notion of temperance. It signifies the ability to withstand inclinations to overindulge our appetites, be they for food and sex or gossip and profanity. Entrepreneurship, known as "industry" among America's Founders, is the virtue that enables us to take risks, work hard, and make smart judgments about what counts as an opportunity and what does not. Whereas the Greeks celebrated courage, the ability to overcome fear in battle, as a complement to temperance, Americans have always celebrated entrepreneurship, the ability to aggressively pursue opportunities in the face of uncertainties, as a complement to restraint.

These four virtues create value in numerous ways for our society—value that is difficult to quantify or estimate. Homes and communities rich in benevolent and just, or fair, actions save our society immeasurable social costs and tend to produce children who are more likely to continue the good work in the future. Children who learn self-control will do less harm to themselves and others. The entrepreneurial, or industrious, create obvious economic value and also produce learning and social improvements that have independent value. These virtues, taken together, give our society a value that is not only economic and utilitarian but moral and social. They give us order without rigidity and flexibility without instability.

They are also universal. That is, as the eminent scholar, James Q. Wilson, points out in *The Moral Sense*, four key moral sentiments—sympathy, fairness, self-control, and duty—which are similar to and supportive of the virtues I present here, are universally promoted by all cultures with only the rarest of exceptions. Wilson argues that the reason so many people today—and especially intellectual elites—are moral relativists is because they have spent their time looking for universal *rules*. Just about any rule governing human behavior admits of exceptions, and thus relativism seems the only logical conclusion. He writes, "I am reckless enough to think that many conducting this search have looked in the wrong places for the wrong things because they have sought for universal rules rather than universal dispositions."[17] The four virtues I present here are rooted in universally accepted dispositions, or sentiments. Because we have a tendency, however weak, to interact with others on the basis of sympathy, fairness, self-control, and obligation, we recognize benevolent, just, restrained, and entrepreneurial behavior as praiseworthy.

Benevolence, justice, restraint, and entrepreneurship cannot be learned through rules, instruction manuals, a business seminar, or graduate school. They are learned by habit and example. Thus, we usually find them wherever we see high levels of interpersonal commitment and responsibility: in healthy families, good communities and neighborhoods, and strong social networks. Each of them is worth thinking about, practicing, and cultivating in our children.

Benevolence

Benevolence is an old word. It is not commonly used today, but it provides us with a good way to say with one word what we usually require several words to describe. It encompasses compassionate acts toward those in need, volunteer activity in civic matters, gifts to charitable and arts organizations, and generosity toward people, organizations, and places with needs in general. Benevolence, which comes from the Latin meaning "good will," is the virtue that prompts us to behave kindly and generously even though no one is forcing us to do so.

It is rooted in the sympathy that we have for others, and for this reason, it is best cultivated in social settings where we come into regular contact with the needs of the community. Wilson writes, "To the extent that benevolence depends on sympathy, benevolence will be bounded by our capacity for sympathy. The more people can enter into the mind of another . . . the more likely they are to be generous to that other."[18]

Benevolence can be exercised and learned through hospitable practices at home. If, as Robert Putnam's research suggests, hospitality is declining in America, we can expect fewer benevolent children in our midst tomorrow. Entertaining at home and casually visiting with friends have been in such a steady decline that Putnam says that they are "on the social capital endangered species list."[19] Research also shows that children in tight-knit rural communities are more apt to practice acts of kindness than their suburban and urban peers.[20] In the midst of benevolence-weakening trends, parents in our mainstream, metro-area culture need to take primary responsibility for exposing their children to benevolent practices by regularly having people into their homes. They cannot rely on a "community," which for most people does not exist as a tight-knit unity, to do this for them.

Benevolence is also regularly learned through volunteering and charitable giving. Religious organizations and houses of worship are essential to American society on this front, since they receive the largest portion of charitable giving in the nation and attract high numbers of volunteers. Hundreds of thousands of additional community-based organizations and community-improvement projects provide outlets for the American impulse to give of time and money.

Just about any community has organizations that could benefit from the talents and goodwill of families that are otherwise sitting at home in front of their televisions and computers (often at the same time in the same home today, given that 77 percent of sixth-graders have televisions in their own rooms, compared to 6 percent in 1970).[21] Children that grow up in homes where sacrificing a night every week for a local charitable cause is standard practice grow up more likely to regard benevolent activity as a normal aspect of a good life.

Justice

It may seem odd to refer to justice as a virtue, and yet until quite recently, this was a basic understanding of the word. It has always referred to the system of laws and principles by which we punish illegal behavior, distribute public goods, and protect established rights. But throughout our history, our most thoughtful leaders have argued that we feel obliged to respect laws of justice in the first place because we have already learned what justice is at home and in our communities. We depend daily on the exercise of justice in our homes, schools, and communities to maintain social order without official laws that force us to do so.

David Hume, for instance, wrote, "Human nature cannot by any means subsist without the association of individuals; and that association never could have place, were no regard paid to the laws of equity and justice . . . . The observance of justice, though useful among [nations], is not guarded by so strong a necessity as among individuals."[22] Justice, Hume argued, is that basic virtue by which people respect each other's property and rights without being forced by law to do so. Justice prompts us to keep promises and hold others accountable for promises they make to us.

We all know, implicitly or explicitly, that we have to live by these basic rules in order to keep our society together, and for this reason, and not vice versa, we respect our institutions of justice such as the police and the courts. People that act unfairly and without responsibility usually feel obligated to provide a reason for their behavior, as if to implicitly acknowledge the moral value of justice. All the more, if a child grows up in an environment rich in trust and respect toward others, he or she will have heightened sensibilities about the importance of justice.

Practicing justice as a virtue means acting fairly toward others, rewarding good behavior, and punishing bad behavior. This is cultivated in several ways. First, environments, whether homes, schools or workplaces, foster justice by encouraging their members to solve problems by considering them from as many angles as possible. This helps people to avoid rushing to conclusions or making prejudiced judgments, which are two of the most common ways of perpetuating injustice.

Second, justice is cultivated by encouraging optimum levels of responsibility in our policies at home, school, the office, or the government. By rewarding our children for helping clean the house they live in, and taking away privileges when they refuse, we instill in them an understanding that they owe something to the community of which they are a part (in this case, the family). This also helps them recognize injustice so that they will speak up for those who are treated unfairly.

Habits of responsibility are also especially important in a society that values property and ownership under the rule of law; these habits give us the ability to understand, operate under, and benefit from our systems of property ownership and property protection. Lastly, habits of justice are cultivated as we learn to come good on the promises and commitments we make to one another. This is more than simple honesty. This is the habit of fulfilling what we say we will do, which builds trust and is the main reason we learn early on why violating contractual agreements is such a serious matter.

Restraint

Societies rely on three mechanisms for controlling behavior that threatens the social order. They pass laws and enforce them; they uphold taboos, which may be legally instituted but are often unofficially enforced through shared customs and beliefs; and they rely upon individual self-control. When self-control erodes, taboos or laws or both may be instituted to control the harm that ensues.

For instance, if too many fathers of Little Leaguers get overly animated on the sidelines on a regular basis, shouting profanities and even coming to blows (this has indeed become something of a problem in some places), other parents may begin ostracizing them in various ways. The league may begin instituting policies that threaten their children's right to participate. And, if things get really bad, the town council may begin passing laws and sending police patrols to the park.

Restraint can only properly be called a virtue when it is found at the level of individual self-control. Complying with taboos and laws is not the same thing as keeping one's passions under check in the absence of those rules. Restraint, as the Greeks envisioned it, was not meant to turn people into prudes. It was intended to equip people to keep their own desires subordinate to the needs of others. It was also intended to help people keep particularly strong desires from dominating them so much that they have nothing to contribute to society. Strong desires—whether for sex, partying, or gossiping—can get out of control, offend others, and ultimately stunt the perpetrator's civic standing. The person who cares about the surrounding community keeps his or her impulses in check.

The lack of restraint is often publicly celebrated as a virtue in our media, even if most people would normally be offended if their neighbors practiced such a "virtue." There is a difference between Howard Stern the radio show host and Howard Stern the dinner guest. The entertainment value of Madonna and Britney Spears gets lost quickly when thirteen-year-old girls begin gyrating and dressing like them at the school dance.

Restraint is thus not simply about saying no to dessert or smoking fewer cigarettes, though it is those things, too. It has a particular social value. It is certainly learned by healthy habits such as avoiding what is bad for us or walking when we feel like sitting. But it is also learned in homes and communities that reinforce two important traits. First, restraint is learned by delaying gratification, most commonly in the context of the values of work. Working, saving, investing—these focus our attention on the future and train us to place restraints on present behavior. Where they are strong, for instance, credit card debt is low.

Delayed gratification is also instilled through families, religious communities, and schools that promote delaying sexual activity. Education and contraceptives may contribute to lowering teen birth rates (though the evidence is not overwhelming), but youth that do not exercise restraint in sexual activity remain highly vulnerable to poverty, hardship, and health risks.

Second, restraint is learned by the promotion of humility—that is, by admitting when we are wrong or do not know something, and by helping those around us feel safe enough to do the same. Intellectual restraint is a virtue too little practiced today, by both the pundit on television and the annoying dinner guest who cannot be told anything he or she does not already know. Humility breeds trust. It also breeds environments where learning and innovation are possible, because the admission of ignorance is fertile soil for intellectual and spiritual growth.

Humility is also a consistent trait of the best corporate CEOs, contrary to conventional wisdom. Jim Collins's groundbreaking research into great companies shows that CEOs who build the best companies take responsibility for corporate failure, praise others for its success, channel ambition into the company rather than the ego, and surround themselves with great talent rather than subordinates who make them look good.[23]

Entrepreneurship

As I mentioned earlier, entrepreneurship is the most widespread form of courage in today's society. Entrepreneurs are not simply the faces that litter the covers of glossy technology and finance magazines. They are small and minority business owners who have decided to risk much in order to provide a better future for themselves and their children. Their activity, secondarily, often benefits the wider community by creating jobs and feeding into the local economy.

Entrepreneurship is a virtue in the same way that writers in the 1700s spoke of "industry." Hume understood happiness as composed of three parts: action, pleasure, and leisure. In its best form action becomes industry, or action aimed at innovating, producing, and gaining. Industrious action imparts vocational purpose and creates the resources by which we undertake a range of enjoyments, whether we take night classes to further our education or simply enjoy a quiet night at home.

A life of "honest industry," Hume writes, "satisfies [the] natural appetites, and prevents the growth of unnatural ones, which commonly spring up, when nourished by ease and idleness."[24] When we have too much free time, whether we are rich or poor, our desires are more likely to get out of balance and take us in directions we do not normally go when we earn our leisure, so to speak, through industrious work and activity. Working diligently and creatively is an important element in the human happiness equation.

Even for the employee—that is, most of us who work without owning or managing our place of work—entrepreneurial behavior is usually rewarded. The employee who works hard, looks for new answers to the same old nagging problems, and optimistically undertakes his or her tasks simply does better over the long run. The industriousness and relentlessness that we usually associate with the entrepreneur are the same traits that employers look for in their employees.

If restraint is partially learned by admitting when we are wrong, entrepreneurship is learned by admitting when we are right. Entrepreneurship demands that we be resolute about our strengths and confident enough to invest in developing them. Entrepreneurs are unabashed about their strong points. Parents, teachers, pastors, and employers can cultivate this type of resolution by allowing failure when young people valiantly try, and by placing them in situations where diffidence about their abilities is not an option.

For the Sake of the Public

The four social virtues reinforce the basic ideals upon which our American democratic republican tradition is built. Namely, they reinforce liberty and equality. They also train us to respond properly to those around us. At times, we need to be reactive; other times, proactive. These virtues, taken together, enable us to navigate the public arena successfully.

Table 8.1: The Four Social Virtues

	Properly Reactive	Properly Proactive
Equality	**Justice**	**Benevolence**
Liberty	**Restraint**	**Entrepreneurship**

Table 8.1 helps make this point. Our shared value of equality places a claim on us to act fairly. We are expected to respond to the acts of others with the virtue of justice. In other words, our society assumes that we will *react* in the right way when a neighbor complains that our new fence violates her property line or

when we learn that a young boy in our neighborhood has been stealing out of neighbors' garages. Justice has an equalizing effect: it keeps our concerns and the concerns of others on roughly the same plane; it judges them by the same standards of fairness. When we fail at justice at home, then the official institutions of justice have to clamp down more firmly.

American society, perhaps more than any other, is built upon a tradition of preserving equality through benevolence. Compared to other countries, we *proactively* expect much of our own kindness and generosity. In the midst of large public programs, Americans experiment with private schools and private voucher initiatives. They launch church-based housing programs and credit counseling. In short, Americans seem driven by the idea that the aims of equality cannot be served by the state alone—or even primarily by the state. We serve the value of equality through our benevolence by helping bring others along. If justice tries to keep people from unfairly rising above the level playing field of society, benevolence tries to help people who are unfairly stuck beneath it.

With regard to liberty, we *react* properly to the freedom of others by restraining our own impulses. Without restraint, we need lots of laws to protect ourselves from ourselves. A society that lacks restraint is like the individual that cannot control his urges: liberty becomes a slave to desire, and freedom is more illusory than real.

We also *proactively* foster liberty in society by being entrepreneurial. Having the courage to take risks and the ability to earn and save money is the road to independence and ownership—in other words, liberty. Where entrepreneurial habits are absent or unrecognized, people are more likely to be dependent on charity or the government. They are less free to raise their children as they wish and are pushed by the necessaries of life instead of the winds of opportunity.

The strength of our future does not rest upon how clear and copious our ethical codes are. Nor does it rest on how zealous we are for our particular ideologies. It rests, rather, upon how well we live out virtues such as the four articulated here. Our civil society is really only as civil as it is virtuous. And it is only as virtuous as its families, congregations, schools, community associations, and enterprises are strong.

Notes

1. Office of Research, Information, and Planning, U.S. Equal Employment Opportunity Commission, Charge Data, 1992-2000, http://www.eeoc.gov/stats/all.html.

2. Dietrich Bonhöffer, *The Cost of Discipleship* (New York: Collier Books, 1963), 45.

3. Jean Bethke Elshtain, *Democracy On Trial* (New York: Basic Books, 1995), 48.

4. Stephen Carter, *Civility: Manners, Morals, and the Etiquette of Democracy* (New York: Basic Books, 1998), 81.

5. David Hume, *Essays Moral, Political, and Literary*, ed. Eugene F. Miller (Indianapolis: Liberty Fund, 1985), 60.

6. Hume, *Essays*, 62.

7. Hume, 27.

8. Immanuel Kant, *Perpetual Peace and Other Essays*, trans. Ted Humphrey (Indianapolis: Hackett, 1983), 127.

9. Gertrude Himmelfarb, "The Idea of Compassion: The British vs. the French Enlightenment," *Public Interest* 145 (Fall 2001): 12.

10. Himmelfarb, "The Idea of Compassion," 13.

11. Himmelfarb, 15.

12. Himmelfarb, 20.

13. C. S. Lewis, *The Abolition of Man, or Reflections on Education with Special Reference to the Teaching of English in the Upper Forms of Schools* (New York: Macmillan, 1955), 34-35.

14. Lewis, *The Abolition of Man*, 35.

15. E. J. Dionne, *Why Americans Hate Politics* (New York; Simon & Schuster, 1991), 10.

16. Aristotle, *Nicomachean Ethics*, trans. Terence Irwin (Indianapolis: Hackett, 1985), 1146a31-35.

17. James Q. Wilson, *The Moral Sense* (New York: Free Press, 1993), 225.

18. Wilson, *The Moral Sense*, 46.

19. Robert Putnam, *Bowling Alone: The Collapse and Revival of American Community* (New York: Simon & Shuster, 2000), 100.

20. Wilson, *The Moral Sense*, 47.

21. Putnam, *Bowling Alone*, 223.

22. David Hume, *Enquiry Concerning the Principles of Morals*, ed. L. A. Selby-Bigge, 2nd ed. (Oxford: Clarendon, 1936), 165.

23. Jim Collins, *Good to Great: Why Some Companies Make the Leap . . . and Others Don't* (New York: HarperCollins, 2001), 22 ff.

24. Hume, *Essays*, 270.

Chapter Nine

The Reformation of Manners

Don Eberly

The abolishment of the British slave trade in 1807 is widely regarded as one of the great turning points in world history. Few, however, know the remarkable details of how it came about, much less what lessons it might hold for today. The campaign to abolish the slave trade lasted from 1787 until 1807, a nineteen-year period during which William Wilberforce introduced the same bill to repeal the trade every year. It would take yet another twenty-six years, until 1833, to fully eradicate slavery from Britain.[1]

Wilberforce was born to aristocracy and entitled to privilege, enormously talented, and encircled by rich and famous friends. Shortly after being elected at the age of twenty-five to the British House of Commons, where he would serve from 1780 to 1825, Wilberforce was urged by a friend to investigate the conditions of slaves. Scandalized and shocked by what he found, and propelled irresistibly forward by a deep religious faith, Wilberforce threw himself at a task that would prove bitterly controversial and recalcitrant: the total abolition of the slave trade.

For Wilberforce, confronting the slave trade meant sacrificing political prestige and upward mobility, enduring ferocious opposition, and facing abruptly ended friendships. Wilberforce's cause would be a popular one today, but in eighteenth-century Britain, slavery was deeply entrenched in the economic system and widely accepted by the public.

For nineteen straight years, well-financed interests and popular resistance handily defeated Wilberforce's legislation. Roughly the size of today's defense industry, the slave trade was a pillar in an empire that traversed the globe. Disruption of the practice threatened not only powerful landowners, merchants, and shipping firms, but also thousands of ordinary laborers such as dockworkers and sailors.

The Linkage of the Abolition of Slavery and Manners

How does abolishing the British slave trade relate to manners? The answer is that the two are inextricably linked. Wilberforce knew that government action against slavery was impossible short of a massive shift in the moral attitudes and habits of the people themselves. On October 28, 1787, Wilberforce wrote in his journal words that would radically alter the course of human affairs, first in Britain and later in America: "God Almighty has set before me two great objects, the suppression of the Slave Trade and the Reformation of Manners."

As impossible as the job of abolishing the slave trade appeared, the remaking of a decadent English society seemed even more daunting. The times were characterized by high rates of crime, drunkenness, and general disregard for moral standards. Public confidence in the laws was at an all-time low, and there was widespread economic and political corruption. The sophisticated classes mocked religion and embraced skepticism toward moral truth as the fashionable outlook while malicious and lewd behavior was commonplace.

Slavery, according to Wilberforce, could not be understood in isolation from these debauched conditions. Moral indifference toward the evil of slavery, he discerned, was nourished in a cultural environment of coarseness and crudeness. The "systematic misery" of slaves was considered but one or two links in the chain removed from the "habitual immorality and degradation" that characterized the masses in society at the time.

By recognizing this linkage, Wilberforce was merely reflecting what others from different places and times in history had observed: that laws are, to a very large extent, a reflection of the culture. Perhaps Edmund Burke offered the most famous encapsulation of this: "Manners are more important than laws. Upon them, in a great measure, the laws depend." Burke continued, manners are "what vex or soothe, corrupt or purify, exalt or debase, barbarize or refine us, by a constant, steady, uniform, sensible operation, like that of the air we breathe in."

This being the case, Wilberforce concluded that to change the law he had to go "upstream" to the tributaries of moral beliefs and conduct. He had to confront the moral ethos in which the slave trade was nourished. Uprooting a corrupt law required reforming the debased culture that legitimated it.

Wilberforce also recognized that, unlike passing antislavery legislation, the work of reforming manners and morals was not the work of the state; such a task would have to be carried out by various voluntary associations within civil society. Over the course of three decades, Wilberforce personally founded, led, or participated in as many as sixty-seven voluntary associations aimed at the reform of manners and morals, resulting in one of the most dynamic chapters in the history of voluntary reform societies. His success at achieving the twin goals—reforming manners and, in turn, eradicating slavery—stands as a monument to the power of voluntary associations and reform societies in bringing social and moral uplift to a debauched culture.

America's Moribund Manners

Whether America has, in its current ill-mannered state, reached the same low-water mark as Britain at the turn of the nineteenth century is open to debate. Judging from the assessment that Americans themselves make of their current condition, it would appear that this is so.

A survey by *U.S. News & World Report* and Bozell Worldwide indicates that many people believe that the behavior of Americans has worsened. Large majorities of Americans feel that their country has reached an ill-mannered watershed. Nine out of ten Americans think incivility is a serious problem, and nearly half think it is extremely serious. Seventy-eight percent say the problem has worsened in the past ten years.[2]

Americans do not see rudeness merely as a private irritant. They see in disrespectful behavior the portends of a more worrisome social disintegration. More than 90 percent of those polled believe incivility and rudeness contribute to the increase of violence in the country; 85 percent believe it divides the national community, and the same number see it eroding healthy values like respect for others.[3]

In other words, the abandonment of responsible behavior is no longer seen as isolated to an occasional episode, nor is it viewed as a matter of merely private concern with no social consequences. It is thought to be both pervasive and affecting the nation's social health.

Pollster George Gallup, who has long tracked American attitudes about values, has "a sinking feeling" when he looks over surveys. A recent Gallup poll showed that a large majority of Americans believe society has "a harsh and mean edge," Gallup says, noting that the United States has become "a society in which the very notion of a good person is often ridiculed," where "retribution is the operative word."[4]

Columnist Michael Kelly describes a "Gresham's law in aesthetics" that operates in our manners just as in economics, which he says works with "breathtaking, ruthless rapidity." Nothing, he says, "is not fit to print," not even the act of the nation's highest leader and chief living symbol of democracy soiling the dress of his adulteress. Kelly proclaims: "The Marxist ideal is at last reached. We live, finally, in a classless society: No one has any class at all."

Kelly sites as evidence of his "classless society" thesis a number of cultural trends which have been adopted by the demographic mainstream, whether fashions or the use of vulgarity. What is remarkable about this, he says, is not that deviance is being used to offend the sensibilities of the refined, which has occurred for centuries, but that deviancy may no longer exist as a category. The offenders are not cultural rebels; they are the mainstream culture. "The horror," he says, "is that we are fast approaching a culture where it is impossible to offend."[5]

Stories of America's slipping manners are regularly captured in our headlines and decried by columnists. Language and behavior standards for film, television, and popular music have eroded to an unprecedented degree. Nearly every community in America has witnessed increased anger and rudeness in public places, to say nothing of road rage occasionally turning violent.[6]

Soccer moms and dads have become so loudmouthed and ill-mannered on the sidelines that one youth soccer league in West Palm Beach has adopted a policy of requiring the parents of all kids who suit up for the game to complete an ethics class. The Juniper-Tequesta Athletic Association, which serves 6,000 kids ages 5-18, is now requiring parents to take an hour-long class in ethical conduct, including training in how to show positive support and good sportsmanship. "We just want to try to de-escalate the intensity that's being shown by the parents at these games," says the volunteer athletic league president.[7]

Few public spaces are not seen as suitable for broadcasting ideas and images once widely thought of as reflecting bad manners. For example, bumper stickers have always been around, advertising one's favorite politician or rock band or promoting a charity or social cause. It has been commonplace to broadcast offbeat ideas and causes via this medium. Today, however, bumper sticker messages carry sexual references and insults, the "F" word, and cartoon characters urinating on anything they find unacceptable.[8]

In an article entitled "A Small Plea to Delete a Ubiquitous Expletive," in *U.S. News & World Report*, Elizabeth Austin plaintively suggests that if American society can agree on nothing else, perhaps establishing the modest goal of removing the now common use of the "F" word from polite circles might be a good start. People, including those who never use bad language, are now forced to hear it frequently "on the street, on the job, at the health club, at the movies—anywhere two or three disgruntled citizens might gather."

Austin adds that the need to work for the elimination of the English language's most vulgar word would have been seen as preposterous a couple of generations ago since neither it nor any comparable word would ever have been used in polite company.[9]

For solutions, Austin recommends that those who use it in their private lives simply stop doing so and that people stop approving of its use. But she also recommends public action. For example, she recommends that police start ticketing drivers who use the word, an action she believes would pass any constitutional test. She further recommends that we be more critical of authors who use it and that the Motion Picture Association of America give an automatic NC-17 rating to any movie that uses the word.

Such an approach still leaves plenty of room for what people are free to say in the locker room or in the privacy of one's home. The rules of civility have always granted a large measure of latitude. Social norms always allow deviation from the norm, although at the price of facing social disapproval from those who still possess taste and moral sensibility. What advocates of manners and civility routinely point out is that the norms themselves—even the idea of commonly accepted norms—have come under assault and are breaking down. A society without civilizing norms will only likely become more brutal and barbaric in time.

More than anything, America is deeply confused and divided over what should be permissible under what circumstances. It's not that Americans aren't outraged, as the polls themselves reflect. It is more the case that, as Lee Bockhorn puts it: "Americans have become schizophrenic about manners." We flock by the millions, he says, "to scatological comedies from the toilet-mouthed *South Park* to the masturbatory *American Pie*." "At the same time," however, "polls reveal that a huge majority believe American manners and morals have undergone a precipitous and deplorable decline."[10] In other words, programming that large majorities of Americans privately report finding deplorable—be it shock radio, soft porn on television, vulgar language, and shockingly degraded movies—is being consumed by sizable numbers of Americans, including many who report finding it offensive.

Manners as Voluntary Rules of Behavior

What Wilberforce understood in his day, and what growing numbers of Americans are coming to appreciate in our own time, is that there is an unbroken link between uncivil and ill-mannered behavior of the milder variety and tolerance for the more barbaric treatment of human beings, illustrated in Wilberforce's time by the slave trade. The corruption of superficial and seemingly harmless behavior can have a far deeper corrupting effect. The attempts by some organizations and movements today to restore civility and recover manners should be seen as an attempt to renew the linkage between freedom and its responsible use with the aid of social rules and restraints. Manners, in other words, serve important purposes in maintaining an ordered freedom in democratic society.

Manners have a unique history as an informal and voluntary tool for shaping individual behavior and social standards. In 1530 the philosopher Erasmus wrote in his etiquette book, *de Civitate*, that a young person's training should consist of four important areas: religion, study, duty, and manners. Another book on manners from the same era, written by French Jesuits in 1595, was translated into English and was adopted by George Washington two centuries later.

John Moulton, a noted English judge, speaking in 1912 on the subject of "law and manners" divided human action into three domains. The domain of law essentially compels people to obey, without much choice in the matter, while the domain of free choice grants the individual unconstrained freedom. Between these two domains lies a third domain that is neither regulated by the law nor free from constraint.

This "domain of obedience to the unenforceable" was what Moulton termed manners. Manners were about proper behavior, of course, but they also entailed a larger concept of moral duty and social responsibility. They involved "doing right where there is no one to make you do it but yourself," where the individual is "the enforcer of the law upon himself."[11]

What Moulton understood was that cultural conditions could not be reversed by government action or changes in the law alone, but by a recovery of manners. Moulton saw the domain of manners as "the whole realm which recognizes the sway of duty, fairness, sympathy, taste, and all others things that make life beautiful and society possible," things which can be easily corrupted but not so easily corrected, at least not by laws.[12]

While the state is in no position to restore manners, the quality of public life and of government is inextricably linked to them. Government is forced to deal with the consequences of the breakdown of manners and moral norms. The erosion of cultural norms practically ensures that the state becomes the arbiter of conflict, and will thus continually expand.

Manners: Small Morals, Limited Government

Every society, to function as a society, must settle on some basic notion of right behavior that is regarded as important and legitimate enough to enforce. Societies have basically two means to enforce right behavior. One is the law, which is a clumsy, heavy-handed, and often inappropriate tool. The second, as Lord Moulton pointed out, is manners. As many observers have pointed out, there is an inverse relationship between the widespread practice of manners and the intrusiveness of law.

When the rules for determining what conduct is proper are no longer set by custom, morality, and religion, the rules of society become decided through politics alone. Judith Martin, a leading etiquette expert, sees manners fulfilling a "regulative" function, similar to that of the law. Where manners function properly, the conscience is informed and behavior is constrained without having to resort to policy or the courts. Martin says that manners work to "soften personal antagonisms, and thus to avert conflicts," so that the law may be restricted to "serious violations of morality."[13] Social rules bring respect and harmony to daily situations.

The wide practice of manners can make the job of governance easier. Political philosopher Thomas Hobbes understood manners as "small morals," and no small protection for a society against what he famously described as "state of nature." Manners were part of the routine of an ordered society, where civility and respect were practiced voluntarily apart from the compulsion of law. They are the bridges between private freedom and public duty.

A system of manners is a way for a free society to induce people to act respectfully by voluntary means. As Hobbes pointed out, manners contribute to the maintenance of order and balance in society: safeguarding society from the nasty, brutish conditions that characterized man in his uncivilized state while minimizing the need for a highly intrusive state.

As individuals make their decisions less and less in accordance with either private conscience or widely accepted moral standards and more on the basis of the law, society becomes legalistic in its approach to behavior; the law, not morality, guides behavior. Under this law-based system of regulating conduct, many are prone to both resort to the law in sorting out differences and to assume that whatever the law does not formally forbid must therefore be permissible. In other words, when the law is the principal arbiter, other gentler forms of regulation—such as ethics and manners—tend to recede.

Judith Martin explains it this way: on the one hand, she says many Americans have come to believe and to put into practice "the idea that any behavior not prohibited by law ought to be tolerated." On the other hand, she says people resort to the law to correct minor offenses that should be socially regulated by manners: "people who found rude but legally permitted behavior intolerable have attempted to expand the law to outlaw rudeness."[13]

Ultimately, says Martin, attempts to eradicate rudeness or obnoxiousness through the law poses a threat "to the freedoms guaranteed by the constitution." Social regulations such as manners not only govern more softly than the law, they are more flexible. Social regulation leaves room for nonconformity, which the law does not, and requires no costly governmental apparatus. The state's rules are absolute and binding, enforceable through arrest and imprisonment. Thus, when conflicts arise in a society governed by a pervasive law rather than social constraints, these conflicts—whether on highways, school playgrounds, or malls—quickly escalate and must be resolved by external authorities. Illustration of this phenomenon at work is the increased number of security personnel serving in locations where they were never needed before, such as in schools and at sporting events.

In many respects this need to balance order and liberty by voluntary means was seen by the American constitutional Framers as the central challenge for the republic, and one which they hoped and expected succeeding generations would take up. The Framers frequently used terms such as habits, dispositions, sentiments, and manners to describe the kind of self-regulating behavior that would maintain public order while minimizing the need for costly, intrusive government.

The constitutional Framers knew they were putting more confidence in the people than might be justified by the experience of history, and that freedom could only be maintained through appropriate order voluntarily maintained by the people. The Founders had little doubt about the durability of the formal framework of constitutional government, but voiced concern about the willingness of the people to undertake the rigors of self-government. The free society requires a capacity not only to regulate one's own passions, but also to have regard for the rights and opinions of others.

The Founders of the American democratic system were attuned to manners and related topics. While they contributed some of the most profound political theory in such documents as the *Federalist Papers*, many of their private writings were filled with references to such things as habits, sentiments, mores, dispositions, and manners. These were the ingredients of a well-ordered society in which individuals took it upon themselves to govern themselves.

At least two Founders, George Washington and Benjamin Franklin, contributed their own original thoughts and writings on manners. As noted earlier, Washington translated onto a small plain notebook 110 "Rules of Civility and Decent behavior in Company and Conversation." In Washington's day, civility was furthered through a set of voluntary rules whereby a person seeking social advancement and distinction learned to display deference to the interests and feelings of others.

Rules of civility were consciously adopted by Washington to win the respect of his fellows and to advance in leadership.[15] By means of a strict code of courteous behavior, Washington established a towering command as a leader on the battlefield. The first principle of manners, according to Washington's rules, had to do with public leadership and conduct: "Every action done in public ought to be done with some sign of respect for those who are present."

Manners and simple courtesy added grace to what was a natural gift for iron-willed leadership. Manners were also the means by which he imposed upon himself self-regulation, ultimately mastering what was widely known to be a severe temper.

Moral Habits Become Internalized

As mentioned above, when rules are established by law they can produce superficial compliance where the person is motivated by avoidance of punishment. By contrast, there is evidence in the case of manners of some internalization of the values. Aristotle held that people are essentially conditioned to be good by developing positive habits, what some modern sociologists refer to as "habituation." He said: "only a blockhead can fail to realize that our characters are the result of our conduct." In other words, people become good by doing good.

Edmund Burke, writing in the eighteenth century, said much the same thing in pointing out that morals, to some extent, depend upon the maintenance of manners. Manners, he said, "give their whole form and color to our lives." "According to their quality," he said, "they aid morals, they supply them, or they totally destroy them."

Mark Caldwell, in his book *A Short History of Rudeness: Manners, Morals and Misbehavior in Modern America,* supplies evidence of this connection between manners and morals, although he says the connection is "deceptive, sinuous, and complicated." He cites a variety of examples in history of how attitudes and beliefs adjusted themselves according to newly expected behavior. For example, the movement to consider racial discrimination unacceptable has led to improved moral attitudes about race. Caldwell concludes that attempts to turn "optional niceties into duties in the hope that this will stiffen our moral spines" has support from the experience of history.[16]

Critics of manners are quick to cast doubt upon this phenomenon by suggesting that rather than supporting moral attitudes, manners are merely a cover for hypocrisy and repression. In other words, manners are discounted as phony because they are thought to bear no relationship to inner character. The defenders of manners will readily admit that hypocrisy is one human behavior that does exist, but quickly add that it is not entirely lacking in social usefulness. Even if the hypocrisy charge is true, a certain amount of what virtue czar Bill Bennett calls "constructive hypocrisy" is necessary because every civilization needs to keep certain perversions under control.[16]

University of Texas associate professor of government J. Budziszewski is among those who believes that practicing courtesy will not only take the edge off some of society's coarseness, it will begin to fundamentally change people. Though courtesy can "mask" some of the unpleasant things one might feel, Budziszewski says this type of mask is not hypocritical, as many would define it, because it has a high purpose. "Masks, of course, can be used to deceive, but in courtesy that is not the aim."[17] It is to guard against wanton disrespect of human beings.

As C. S. Lewis, Gilbert Meilaender, and a host of other scholars and social critics have explained, masks are worn partly in hopes that our true faces will gradually grow to fit them, and partly to set a good example in the meantime. "If you please," "thank you," and "the pleasure is mine" may be mere formulae, says Budziszewski, but "they rehearse the humility, gratitude and charity that I know I ought to feel and cannot yet." Courtesy, he says, finds its place in a world where people "would like to be better than they are."[18]

Cultural Forces behind the Corruption of Manners

The wide acceptance of manners has always waxed and waned throughout society. Their waning in recent decades has been brought about by cultural and philosophical influences, some of which may have been inherent in the American system from the beginning, and some of more recent origins.

Alexis de Tocqueville praised many aspects of the American system of democracy, especially its driving impulse toward equality, but wondered how a society that would do away so completely with social distinctions could preserve a sense of mutual respect and obligation when it came to social conduct. Tocqueville speculated that America's incessant drive toward equality would produce a dynamic, opportunity-rich society, but that it would do so at the expense, in effect, of manners. He warned that Americans would use their freedom not merely for purposes of individual industry but in pursuit of "petty and paltry pleasures."

Another factor of more recent origins is the weakening of those institutions, which typically transmit manners and morals. Michael Sandel states that worries about incivility express a deeper fact that the moral fabric of community is unraveling around us. "From families and neighborhoods to cities and towns to schools, congregations and trade unions, the institutions that traditionally provided people with moral anchors and a sense of belonging are under siege."[19]

As Sandel and others argue, it is not enough to have a clear concept of what manners and morals are. They depend upon effectively functioning value-shaping institutions, with real legitimacy and authority, to be transmitted. "You can't have strong virtues without strong institutions," says University of Chicago ethics professor Jean Bethke Elshtain, "and you can't have strong institutions without moral authority." [20]

The erosion of authority and community norms picked up momentum in recent decades as an ideology of individual autonomy became widely embraced in the culture, the objective of which has been to liberate the individual from all inner as well as outer restraints, including commonly held social standards.

Much of the authority that was once enjoyed by family, religion, and the civic community has been transferred to the individual. Says Allen Ehrenhalt, "there may be a welter of confused values operating in the 1990s, but there is one point on which all Americans speak with unity and unmistakable clarity." We have become, he says, "emancipated from social authority as we once used to know it."[21] This is true, says Ehrenhalt, throughout every segment of America, whether the urban ghetto or the middle or upper classes of America, and it is grounded in an excessive orientation toward individual autonomy. The worship of individual autonomy and the suspicion of authority "has meant the erosion of standards of conduct and civility, visible mostly in the schools where teachers who dare to discipline pupils risk a profane response."[22]

A culture that is in search of greater emancipation from all restraints is likely to see such things as manners as a barrier, not an aid, to individual development. Says William Bennett "the messages being so powerfully promulgated is basically this: the *summum bonum* of life is self-indulgence, self-aggrandizement, instant gratification; the good life is synonymous with license and freedom from all inhibitions; rules are undesirable and made to be broken; and self-fulfillment is achieved by breaking them."[23]

Repudiating an Older Culture of Conformity

Some would say that the erosion of social standards over the past several decades is an understandable, if somewhat excessive reaction, to a culture that previously erred on the side of a conformity that stifled individual expression. The excessively constrictive standards of the 1950s were thrown off by the "baby boom" generation, which is now demographically dominant. For many in this generation, the call to manners cannot be confused with a return to a previous era with all of its limits and social rigidity. Many in this generation have second thoughts about the social revolution they spawned, but few are willing to go back to where things were.

And how different those social standards were. Writing in the fall of 1996 in the *Wilson Quarterly*, James Morris describes films from the postwar era that show Americans in public places, like baseball games, almost as though "they're under the sway of an alien force. The women wear blouses and skirts or dresses or, more formal still, suits—and hats, hats, hats. The men are suited too, and hatted row after row to the horizon with brimmed felt jobs, deftly creased." Rules were set by people in communities, not the halls of Congress: "The kids you were told not to play with, the people who could not be invited to dinner, the topics that could never be discussed, the Sears-sized catalogue of actions that were 'shameful' and 'unforgivable' and 'unmentionable.'"

Morris doubts Americans will exchange the present for a past considered "speciously safe, ignorant and restricted." Manners depend on acknowledging authority, but authority is hard to come by in "a vigorous strutting democracy." No one, Morris adds, "wants to make a judgment, to impose a standard, to act from authority and call conduct unacceptable." Until standards of intelligence and behavior are defined and defended once again, "we had better be prepared to live with deterioration."[24] Modern skepticism toward moral values has reduced what was once widely considered objective standards of morality to matters of personal taste, preference, and individual choice.

If the 1950s were stifling, as most would agree, Morris says the present age is its radical opposite. "In this age of 'whatever,' Americans are becoming slaves to the new tyranny of nonchalance." For thirty years every facet of the culture has steadily coarsened. Movies, music, television, newspapers, and magazines dwelt routinely on topics that, according to Morris, were "once too hot for whispers."

An older culture of almost stoic self-denial, which erred on the side of restraint, has been traded in for a culture of self-realization and sensuality in which there are no universal values to which all consent, only individual preferences and desires. Popular culture broadcasts this new tendency by encouraging everyone to ignore the rules. Calvin Klein targets secularized images of youth as "people who do only what they want to do." Saab sells cars by telling us to "peel off inhibitions; find your own road." Nintendo urges children to "be heard; play it loud" as a boy spits at the camera. Healthy Choice Cereals suggests that to be happy "you gotta make your own rules."

If manners are about anything, they are about concealment of what is private, especially one's body and its functions. Manners, much like clothing for the body, provide an outer covering of unpleasant or debased tendencies. Most will acknowledge that up until perhaps the mid-twentieth century, American culture encouraged people to repress aberrant thoughts and behaviors. Now, says James Wolcott, "the problem is the opposite; getting people to put a cork in it. What was once quite possible to accomplish has become impossible to stop." Even our deepest darkest secrets, "our once hidden shames," become easy pickings for publicity hounds. Because popular culture is now filled with "so many memoirs covering so many addictions and afflictions, the confessions have gotten kinkier and more gossipy, as writers add extra salsa to stand out from the growing herd."[25]

In this environment, to be well-mannered is to appear to engage in repression toward oneself. To expect manners of others is to risk appearing moralistic and judgmental. Wendy Shalit, a scholar and author who is attempting to restore public support for modesty, states that "compunction is not a dysfunction." Reacting to the appearance of the completely naked, pregnant body of super model Cindy Crawford on the cover *of W Magazine*, Shalit observes: "Cindy Crawford declares that she is 'comfortable with her body' and shows it to the whole world. But there is good reason to protect the private realm and keep sex sacred: not because you are ashamed but, on the contrary, because you want to reveal yourself only to the one who loves you."[26]

Closely linked to manners is the capacity for shame and the desire to achieve respectability. Amitai Etzioni, founder of the communitarian movement, recommends the use of shame in confronting antisocial behavior, for example by publishing the names of men who solicit prostitutes; requiring drunk drivers to have labels on their license plates; or even dunce caps for serious troublemakers. "Like any other tool, it can be abused, but that doesn't make it wrong in principle. Compared to jail, shame is a very benign tool."[27]

The loss of interest in manners can be tied directly to declining concern about respectability in any number of areas, including such basic things as fashions. For example Mark Caldwell describes designer jeans as "a skeleton key to the mystery of manners." For the lower classes, the jeans are merely tacky. For others, however, the imitation of their economic inferiors becomes a social statement. In other words a lowering of dress standards and a lowering of manners and language can and do go hand in hand.

The Anonymous Society

Another factor in the loss of manners is the speed and rootlessness of modern life. People are less inclined to worry about manners when they aren't personally known, or when they are under pressure. People may simply have less time to be well-mannered, says Ted Anthony. "Technology, mass media, and a desire to do more, do it better and do it yesterday have turned us into hurriers." He describes the twentieth century as "a hundred year madness": "it started with horses and hours. It ends with Maseratis and microseconds, with cars speeding across highways, airplanes streaking across skies, microprocessors burning across desktops. This century's mad dash of innovation has produced all of these things—and the most frantic human era ever." "This overwhelming desire to get from A to B, it's madness," causing us to be oblivious to one another.[28]

Technology itself, which is driving this accelerating process, may be a factor in our declining regard for others. Says David Masci: "Something as frivolous as a walkman brings millions of people pleasure every day. But by shutting out the people we encounter on the street, we inhibit an essential piece of what we think of as our humanity. Compassion, generosity, and empathy are all in part tied to our ability to find common ground with those around us. And it is much harder to find common ground without common courtesy."[29]

Added to speed is the anonymity that exists in a transient, uprooted society. Americans simply don't know each other the way they did when they had less busy lives and when most lived in one community for a lifetime. "Hello" and "excuse me" are less likely to be said among perfect strangers. When you know fewer people, the world is bound to appear riskier. According to Mark Caldwell, "Learning manners and living with their consequences would be easy if people and their social systems would only stay put. Most group relations are never stable anywhere; America is and always has been more volatile than the world average." Mobility and the technology that made it possible, says Caldwell "heightened civilization in one way, but put the skids to it in others."

Renewal Movements

Periodically throughout American history, society has realized the importance of "the unenforceable" social rules and embraced renewal movements to revive them. In nineteenth-century America, for example, books and manuals for the application of manners to every aspect of life flourished. One bibliography assembled during this period counted 236 separate titles on manners.[30] When Emily Post's famous book, *Etiquette,* was published in 1922, it became such a publishing success that it rivaled Sinclair Lewis's *Babbit,* also published that year.

Today's manners movement has arisen in very much the same fashion. Manners are offered as at least a partial corrective to the excesses of a generation that spent its youth determined to throw off social conventions and constraints. A growing interest in manners is reflected in the popularity of books on the subject and a widening network of civility advocates. These contemporary authors carefully avoid appearing stiff or Victorian, and instead link manners to a widely expressed desire for greater social harmony and mutual respect.

Modern-day manners philosopher Judith Martin, who has written extensively on the subject, says manners are defined as that "part of our fundamental beliefs or wants that include such notions as communal harmony, dignity of the person, a need for cultural coherence, and an aesthetic sense."[31] Etiquette is the set of rules that emerges from these fundamental beliefs.

Evidence that a search is on for more civilized social customs can be found in the popularity of films, such as the Jane Austen series, based in highly mannered societies where the characters suppress their emotions and urges, and express fastidious regard for others. Further evidence can be found in the astonishing success of *The Rules,* a runaway bestseller which establishes for women new (actually old) rules of conduct in courtship in order to secure the respect and fidelity of one's suitor. *The Rules,* says Maggie Gallagher, "violate the most sacred precepts of the 1960s about sex and love: that men and women are the same; that love means letting it all hang out; that people shouldn't play games." By games, she meant essentially the rules of polite romantic encounter, grounded in mutual respect and mannerly conduct.

The return to manners reflects a growing awareness that the loss of standards in courtship have been costly, especially to women. In her book *A Return to*

Modesty, Ruth Shalit describes the dreadful consequences of declining respect for women in areas of courtship and sex, and predicts a counterrevolution in women's attitudes: "In the face of all the cultural messages that bark at them that promiscuity and exhibitionism are liberation, they are slowly but surely coming to think the opposite."

Promoting the rules of respect may also be good for commerce. Sensing that courtesy might strengthen the city's tourism industry, New York City civic leaders launched a campaign to encourage its citizens to be nicer to the 25 million people who visit the city each year. "Instead of Making a Wise Crack, Smile," the campaign encourages, and "Turn your Back on Tourists and They'll Turn Their Backs on New York." Thanks to the program, cabbies get a new supply of air fresheners, while cops, airport personnel, and subway workers get sensitivity training.

The history of manners suggests that they inevitably rebound when conditions require them, as if by some law of nature. Mark Caldwell describes an "innate and unconscious human law" that seems to conserve manners, even against the odds. He observes that as the Internet has already begun to demonstrate, even a social space created with conscious lawlessness quickly demonstrates a need for order and generates a rough code of manners."[32]

Conclusion

Over the course of his decades-long campaign to renew English society, Wilberforce created, led, or participated in at least sixty-seven benevolent societies which promoted the social reformation in dozens in dozens of areas, including public health, aid to the poor, education reform, and the humane treatment of animals.

Some societies were religious, some secular, including the Society for the Reformation of Manners. When William Wilberforce set out to reform the manners and morals of the people he did not draft legislation or form a political action committee. There was already plenty of that. Instead, he collaborated with social reformers in developing society-wide campaigns to effect attitudes and behavior.

Proclamations promoting public virtue had been issued annually by King George III, but widely ignored. Wilberforce persuaded the king to reissue one such proclamation, bearing the ungainly name "Proclamation for the Encouragement of Piety and Virtue and for the Preventing of Vice Profaneness and Immorality." This time, Wilberforce decided to accompany the proclamation with the creation of local "societies" for the purpose of reforming manners in localities all across England.

Wilberforce added real community-based campaigns to an otherwise abstract and largely ignored official declaration, and the result was an elevation of the people's conduct and refinement of their tastes. The reform campaigns provided direct help to "persons of dissolute and debauched lives." The theory behind these reform societies was that seemingly small things, including manners, matter. Minor offenses against the common good were seen as the fertile ground for more serious crime.

Wilberforce's many councils were usually organized around odd bedfellows and peculiar coalitions. Wilberforce insisted that his "measures, not men" motto would be the means by which persons of all persuasions and stations in life could be recruited to his social reform movement.

Notes

1. An earlier abbreviated version of the present chapter appeared as "The Reformation of Manners," in *Building a Healthy Culture: Strategies for an American Renaissance*, ed. Don Eberly (Grand Rapids: Eerdmans, 2001). Permission to reproduce this essay in its present form has been generously granted by Eerdmans Publishing Company.

2. John Marks, "The American Uncivil Wars," *U.S. News & World Report*, April 22, 1996, 67-68.

3. Marks"The American Uncivil Wars."

4. Don E. Eberly, "Civil Society: The Paradox of American Progress," *Essays on Civil Society* 1, no. 2 (January 1996), 2..

5. Michael Kelly, "The Age of No Class," *Washington Post*, August 11, 1999, A19.

6. Associated Press, "Man Dies After Road Rage Attack," November 23, 1999.

7. Associated Press, "Loudmouth Parents Must Take Ethics Course for Kids' Games," November 18, 1999.

8. Gil Smart, "Bumper Sticker Shock," *Lancaster Sunday News*, Lancaster, Pa, November 11, 1999.

9. Elizabeth Austin, "A Small Plea to Delete A Ubiquitous Expletive," *U.S. News & World Report*, April 6, 1988, 58.

10. Lee Bockhorn, "Do Manners Matter?" *Weekly Standard*, August 16, 1999, 36.

11. John Silber, "The Media and Our Children: Who Is Responsible," *Windgate Journal*, from Boston University Commencement Address (May 1995), 11-13.

12. Roger Kimball, "You Are Not Excused," *Wall Street Journal*, July 13, 1999.

13. Judith Martin and Gunther S. Stent, "I Think; Therefore I Thank: A Philosophy of Etiquette," *American Scholar*, 59 (Spring 1990): 245.

14. Judith Martin, "The Oldest Virtue," in *Seedbeds of Virtue: Source of Competence, Character and Citizenship in American Society*, ed. Mary Ann Glendon and David Blankenhorn (Lanham, Md.: Madison Books, 1995), 67.

15. Richard Brookhiser, *Rules of Civility: The 110 Precepts that Guided Our First President in War and Peace* (New York: Free Press, 1997).

16. Bockhorn, "Do Manners Matter?," 36.

17. Jonathan Alter, "Next: 'The Revolt of the Revolted,'" *Newsweek*, November 6, 1995, 46.

18. J. Budziszewski, "The Moral Case for Manners," *National Review*, February 20, 1995, 64.

19. Budziszewski, "The Moral Case for Manners," 62.

20. Michael J. Sandel, "Making Nice is Not the Same as Doing Good," *New York Times*, December 29, 1996.

21. Kenneth L. Woodward, "What is Virtue?," *Newsweek*, June 13, 1994, 38.

22. Allen Ehrenhalt, "Learning From The Fifties," *Wilson Quarterly* (Summer 1995): 19.

23. Ehrenhalt, "Learning from the Fifties," 8.

24. From "Images of Ourselves: Washington and Hollywood," a speech by William Bennett to the Center for the Study of Popular Culture, February 24, 1996.

25. James Morris, "Democracy Beguiled," *Wilson Quarterly* (August-September, 1996): 24.

26. James Wolcott, "Dating Your Dad," *New Republic*, March 31, 1997, 32.

27. Ruth Shalit, "Dysfunction Junction," *New Republic*," April 14, 1997, 24.

28. Jonathan Alter, "The Name of the Game is Shame," *Newsweek*, December 12, 1994, 41.

29. Ted Anthony, "Speed," *Lancaster Sunday News,* Lancaster, Pa., January 10, 1999.

30. David Masci, "A Lesson in Civility," *Washington Times*, September 25, 1995.

31. Morris, , "Democracy Beguiled," 24.

32. Martin and Stent, "I Think," 245.

33. Bockhorn, "Do Manners Matter?" 36.

Chapter Ten

The Golden Rule
A Universal Moral Ethic for Society

Don Eberly

Much of the world appears to be searching for a framework of moral belief uniquely relevant to our time and circumstances: one that is positive and inspiring, one that is universally acceptable and thus unifying, one that is grounded in spiritual principles but nonsectarian, and one that is general enough to be adopted not only by every sector of our own society but quite possibly by all societies in an increasingly interconnected globe.

The quest for new beginnings in the area of social ethics is not new for Americans. There are numerous examples of occasions in America's past when periods of moral and ethical loosening were followed by periods of constraint and reform. Each period tends to focus on a particular principle that draws people together from diverse backgrounds. During one such period, the late nineteenth century, American business, civic, and political leaders turned to the Golden Rule as a universal ethic to guide the moral renewal of society. The question addressed by this chapter is whether the Golden Rule might be uniquely suited to meeting similar conditions today.

Evidence of the need for this ethical foundation within American society is seen in the continuing trend toward incivility and rudeness and pervasive confusion over the moral rules by which a free and voluntary society should be governed. Large majorities of the general public have registered consistent concerns over the erosion of social values and the thinning out of civic institutions. Citizens widely report being concerned about the decline of neighborliness and an unwillingness of many of their fellow citizens to rise above self-interest.

Pollster Daniel Yankelovich observes that the most consequential transformation in our culture has come from large numbers of people moving from an attitude of "duty to others" to a sense of "duty to self." [1] This perception that too many people are out for themselves is generating strong support for a higher set of social standards focusing, once again, on the qualities of respecting and caring for one another.

Those who would seek to confront our cultural conditions must acknowledge the uniqueness of current American attitudes about moral life if they wish to succeed. Americans see both these social maladies and the solution to them located in the context of civil society. Americans do not believe that moral life will be renewed through divisive rhetoric or strategies relying on legislative or governmental cures for cultural problems.

By contrast, efforts that promote moral renewal by means of persuasion and consensus-building and within the voluntary sector of civil society—our voluntary associations, neighborhoods, civic organizations, places of worship and popular culture—enjoy wide public support. The American people believe values must be restored in our homes, schools, workplaces, and communities.

Searching for the Ethical Unity amid Ethnic Diversity

Like never before, the human race needs common principles for the ordering of social and moral life. Two great tides are simultaneously affecting the human race at the dawn of the twenty-first century: one, the continued rapid movement toward greater ethnic and religious pluralism combined with wider technological and commercial integration as a global community; and two, the rise of profoundly complex ethical challenges across the globe. The question becomes: what universal principle might exist to which a majority of the world's diverse populations, both secular and religious, might consent for encouraging civilized human conduct?

Coming to agreement over common values can be difficult. These moral debates can divide. But no one can deny that all societies need a moral code. Political and moral philosopher Vaclav Havel, who spent his life searching for ways to recover moral transcendence, first as a writer and then as president of the Czech Republic, believes that human civilization will only be possible if "we all accept a basic code of mutual coexistence, a kind of common minimum we can all share, one that will enable us to go on living side by side." [2]

That "common minimum" may look different in today's society in which Muslims outnumber Episcopalians in American society and whites will be an ethnic minority by mid-century. Much of the moral and philosophical grounds for America's social system originated on European soil, but the foundational principles of justice and virtue transcend particular religious traditions and ethnic backgrounds. They are rooted in natural laws that can be discerned and applied by humankind anywhere.

Havel maintains that while we may need to continue to expand the combined traditions of classical, Judaic, and Christian belief systems, we must find somewhere in the foundations of religions and cultures "respect for what transcends us; certain imperatives that come to us from heaven, or from nature, or from our own hearts; a belief that our deeds will live after us; respect for our neighbors, for our families, for certain natural authorities; respect for human dignity and for nature; a sense of solidarity and benevolence towards guests that come with good intentions."[3]

Many observers believe that progress toward a global spiritual and moral renewal has been stymied during recent decades because of our collective failure to recover positive moral principles that can be universally applied. However, as numerous trends indicate, people across the globe believe that precisely these principles can and must be discovered and widely applied in our lives.

The search for moral foundations can be found today in the renewed interest being expressed in religion and spirituality, including faith-based social policies, increased popularity of character education, and search for manners and basic ethical rules for living. Whereas the search for happiness was until recently assumed to take society in ever more secular directions, most now acknowledge that achieving personal health and happiness, not to mention social harmony and global progress, will require the embrace of universal "laws of life."

Another challenge to recovering moral consensus is a set of American tendencies usually described under the rubric of individualism. Embracing a moral order larger than the individual is difficult when much of the language of society focuses on the rights and entitlements of the private, individual self, not individuals bound together by common needs. Thus individualism has come under increased focus as a leading cause of declining social cohesion and civic decline.

While the United States has always placed a premium on the individual, perhaps more so than any civilization, the individualism of today is thought of as more extreme. What must be recognized is that two forms of individualism have vied for acceptance. One "is moral, ultimately grounded in religion, according to which life is sacred and each person is unique, irreplaceable and priceless; the other is rational and utilitarian, in which the social good is whatever best satisfies the preferences of individual actors."[4]

This latter form of utilitarian individualism, combined with moral relativism, has not been friendly to the institutions of civil society, according to most observers. In fact, the pervasive moral skepticism and doubt of our time comes as close as any other factor to being the chief cause of near collapse of authority and legitimacy that institutions need to function in a society. Since the 1960s, says Amitai Etzioni, "many of our traditions, social values and institutions have been challenged, often for valid reasons," but he adds, the end result is that "we live in a state of increasing moral confusion and social anarchy."[5]

Much of the impetus behind these chaos-producing trends is a philosophical utilitarianism that may be leading the United States away from the possibility of a peaceful and enduring public order.

Golden Rule: Positive, Universal, and Practical

If there is a principle that might serve as the keystone to a new moral framework it is the Golden Rule. At the same time moral and utilitarian, universal and particular, spiritual and temporal, the Golden Rule is one of the best principles for wide application, and quite possibly the best chance for a breakthrough solution in a world searching for moral cohesion. Everyone seems to want more character, more civility, and more responsibility. But merely desiring these things is not enough. One must ask: what is the basic moral principle that might form the basis of a new social ethos in which all of those positive habits are widely recovered and practiced?

The chief advantage of the Golden Rule is that it transcends cultures, particular moral codes, and religious creeds and confessions. The Golden Rule is codified in every major and minor world religion and is embraced by Eastern and Western philosophies alike. Sir John Templeton, a longtime advocate of the Golden Rule, writes, "There must be something powerfully effective in the Golden Rule because its guidance, perhaps with slightly different phrasing, is found in every major religion and regarded as one of the basic spiritual principles of life." It is also supported by the vast majority of the nonreligious, making it the potential keystone of a universal social covenant.[6]

The Power of Positive, Life-Affirming Morality

The Golden Rule offers distinct advantages as the foundation of social ethics when compared to other approaches and ethical principles. Many current attempts to restore values and character have one or another of the following flaws. (1) They are too complex or abstract. (2) They are too elitist and not accessible enough for the masses. (3) They simply do not enjoy a near-universal consensus.

Many approaches to moral uplift fail for a more basic reason: they are simply too negative to inspire the sympathies of the people. Morality must be more than a negative proposition. There is a time and place for moral rules to be presented in the negative—"don't do this, don't do that," "control your impulses," "obey the rules," "don't act selfishly or rudely." But moral life must be more than an affair of imposition and enforcement, says Jeffery Wattles, author of *The Golden Rule* and a leading authority on ethics. It must be more than "a cultural voice that says 'no'." According to Wattles, "Morality comes to its highest fruition in a life devoted to truth, beauty, and goodness on material, intellectual, and spiritual levels."

Character education expert Thomas Lickona agrees that moral objectives often present morality as a set of negative propositions or obligations. They play an essential role because they tell us "for the most part what not to do." But this "prohibitive morality," as he describes it, is not enough. "A responsibility ethic supplies the vital giving side of morality." Says Lickona: "The call to 'love your neighbor' and 'think of others' is open-ended; it doesn't tell us how much we should sacrifice for our families, give to charitable causes, work for our communities, or be there for those who need us. But a morality of responsibility does point us in the right direction. Over the long haul it calls us to try, in whatever way we can, to nurture and support each other, alleviate suffering, and make the world a better place for all."[7]

The other issue that surfaces in regard to promoting moral rules is the issue of penalties versus rewards. This was the genius of successful approaches to inspiring moral behavior in the past. The objective of *The McGuffey's Readers*, for example, was to employ stories and examples of heroism to kindle a desire for honesty, kindness, faithfulness, and courage. *The McGuffey's Readers* offered children direct moral advice based upon the Golden Rule. "Always do to other children as you wish them to do to you. This is the Golden Rule. So remember it when you play. Act upon it now, and when you are grown up, do not forget it."[8]

The moral life is life affirming and conducive to happiness and success. But the moral life requires affirming. Moral affirmation in today's lax climate requires recovering a "moral voice," one that does not merely censure, but which "blesses," says Amitai Etzioni. It is time to reconstruct social values, says Etzioni, not along the lines of merely asserting authority such as in the 1950s, but along lines which nevertheless have us once more providing "moral affirmation."[9] We affirm moral action in community when "we appreciate, praise, recognize, celebrate and toast those who serve their communities, from volunteer fire fighters to organizers of neighborhood crime watches."[10]

In other words, principled living flourishes when it arises out of a positive quest for the good life, or for the joys of life which are the common aim of all. Understood this way, the Golden Rule is embraced as an aid to individual growth and, in its wider application, the source of social progress. It presents itself as a formula for acting upon existing moral aspirations and a widely shared vision for social progress. The Golden Rule facilitates the development of higher forms of living at the emotional, intellectual, and spiritual levels. The primary merit of the Golden Rule is that it serves as a principle—broad, positive, and general—for application in the arena of practical ethics, both personal and social, national as well as international.

The final advantage of the Golden Rule is that it appeals to one's natural sense of self-interest, practical utility, and reciprocity. Unlike the claims of religious creeds or of binding moral truths, the Golden Rule can serve as the basis of a modern social covenant because it appeals to the wide tendency within modernity to consider the utilitarian value and actual life-giving benefits of principles. Rather than summoning individuals to the moral life strictly on the basis of moral "ought" or obligation, the Golden Rule is grounded equally in the enlightenment principle of rational self-interest and personal choice. Some may choose to apply the Golden Rule as a life ethic out of self-transcending love of others; many more may do so in the rational expectation that acts of mercy and kindness will be justly reciprocated.

The Intellectual Challenge to Moral Foundations

One might ask how society got to this point of confusion over foundational moral principles in American society. Those who have analyzed the evolution of moral thought in Western societies, and particularly in America, point to several powerful currents that have eroded moral consensus.

One influence, of course, is the state of moral philosophy generally within influence centers of American society, especially universities. Modern philosophy, says eminent political scientist James Q. Wilson, author of *The Moral Sense*, with some exceptions, represents a fundamental break with philosophical traditions of the past that held individuals capable of, and responsible for, acting morally toward one another. For the past century, he says, "few of the great philosophical theories of human behavior have accorded much weight to the possibility that men and women are naturally endowed with anything remotely resembling a moral sense." In recent years, Wilson maintains that moral philosophy fell to a "relentlessly materialistic doctrine in which morality, religion and philosophy have no independent meaning."[11]

In this materialistic universe, people are understood to have instincts and appetites, but no "moral sense," no moral law written on their hearts, no innate conscience. Freud, Marx, and behaviorism hold man to be little more than a product of the incentives that operate upon him in the environment.

Aiding in this twentieth-century process of undermining objective moral principles was a philosophical doctrine of Logical Positivism, which sought in the name of objective scientific inquiry to establish a radical distinction between facts and values. Facts existed in the objective realm of research and observation. Values were assigned to the subjective category of feelings, preferences, and tastes. This attitude became especially pervasive in educational fields as schools and universities could find no basis for including a place for morality within secular sciences. Values were thought to be inherently unscientific, more akin to religious faith. Moral education was thus perceived to involve indoctrination, and thought of as entirely inconsistent with principles of cultural diversity and intellectual objectivity.

Sources of Morality: The Return to Natural Law

Given the doubt and confusion that immediately surrounds an effort to "revive" or "restore" moral values, questions regarding the source of morality must be taken seriously. Confusion over what moral education and character development can contribute turn quickly to arguments over the question of whose values should be upheld? To what authoritative sources do we turn for moral guidance?

Religious Belief and Practice

One source of moral principles, and by far the most widely understood, is religious belief. Religious believers are usually quite clear on what is ethically right and wrong, and they do not need laws to guide their conduct across a host of behaviors—violence, killing, or simply being unkind to people, for example. They are motivated to do good and avoid evil, not merely to comply with a public law or please people, but because there are divine sanctions which they violate at the risk of their own souls.

But while religion is an important influence and its place within public institutions and places is always being debated, advocates of religiously grounded morality often make the mistake of implying that there are no other foundations for moral life outside of revealed religion. Moreover, efforts to revive public morality based upon religious appeals can quickly be dismissed as sectarian, the effect of which is to mobilize those who think the moral enterprise is faulty on church-state grounds. Religious foundations for moral life are important, especially in a society so thoroughly religious as America, but they are not the only foundations.

Universal Moral Principles: Natural Law

One can explore every corner of the globe and every segment of the human race and find remarkable unanimity regarding what is philosophically called "the good." Even where vast cultural differences exist, there is little disagreement over the characteristics of a good person, a good neighbor, a good community, or a good society. No one wants to be treated discourteously, much less barbarously.

Many moral claims are self-evidently true: for example, that honesty and kindness are good, and that a long series of offenses against mankind and nature are wrong: murder, slavery, sexual exploitation, spouse or child abuse, slaughtering endangered species, or dumping toxic substances into streams. These things are simply wrong, anywhere and under all circumstances. There is no known society in the world that does not consider Mother Teresa a saintly hero, and Hitler a heinous murderer. Things may blur a bit when we enter less clearcut categories, but the point here is that moral assertions have always been made, and must be made.

John M. Cooper offers this summary:

> The peoples of the world, however much they differ as to details of morality, hold universally, or with practical universality, to at least the following basic precepts. Respect the Supreme Being or the benevolent being or beings that take his place. Do not "blaspheme." Care for your children. Malicious murder or maiming, stealing, deliberate slander, or "black lying, when committed against friend or unoffending fellow clansman or tribesman, are reprehensible.

> Adultery proper is wrong, even though there are may be exceptional circum-
> stances that permit or enjoin it and even though sexual relations among the
> unmarried may be viewed leniently. Incest is a heinous offense. This universal
> moral code agrees rather closely with our own Decalogue taken in a strictly
> literal sense."[12]

For those concerned that a system of values cannot be constructed or taught without favoring one religion or culture over another, they have not considered the support that various faith traditions, operating within diverse cultural settings, have given to moral principles.

Support for natural law and natural morality can be found in all religious traditions. C. S. Lewis, himself a devout Christian, pointed out in *The Abolition of Man* that there are certain universal ideas of right and wrong that recur in the writings of ancient Egyptians, Babylonians, Hebrews, Chinese, Norse, Indians, and Greeks, along with Anglo-Saxon and American writings. Lewis called these transcendent principles the Tao, a term borrowed from the Chinese that means simply "the way."

Rooted in the laws of nature, the Tao is a road that leads to the good life, and to harmony with nature and its maker. The concept bases such moral imperatives as the care for the young and veneration of the old, not on subjective human psychology, but in universal principles of justice that transcend individuals and cultures.

Among these universal laws, according to Lewis, are the laws of beneficence, of justice, of good faith and veracity, of mercy, of magnanimity, and of duty to family. That these core principles emerged around the globe and throughout the millennia, independent of one another, on vastly different soil, producing the same successful civilizations regardless of race or religion, confirms Lewis's suggestion that they are rooted in natural laws of the universe, not just Judeo-Christian doctrines found in divine revelation, for example.

These universal principles embodied what Lewis called "a common human law of action which can overreach rules and ruled alike." Belief in the Tao is necessary to "the very idea of a rule which is not tyranny."[13] To abandon them, says Lewis, is to sap a civilization of its dynamism, creativity, and coherence. When societies abandon the Tao, according to Lewis, they produce "men without chests," of whom society vainly expects "virtue and enterprise." To step outside the Tao, says Lewis, is to have "stepped into the void"—it is socially suicidal.[14]

The common core virtues that Lewis identifies are not ethnocentric; they span time, cultures, and religions. Many of the purveyors of these human values on the American continent, though European and predominantly Christian, were drawing from a deeper and more diverse well of antiquity than simply European culture. Thus, rather than magnifying differences, the recovery of moral principles that transcend cultures can be applied as the answer to a divisive multiculturalism. The rich heritage and contributions of all immigrant groups can be honored, and no group has a monopoly on virtue or a special exemption from human vice.

America is witnessing something of a revival of interest in the logic and practicality of natural law. Natural law expert Professor J. Budziszewski, states that "Natural Law" appears in the title of at least twenty-six books published in America over the past two years.[15]

Morality in Our Common Experience

Yet another foundation for ethics can be found in a search for core principles or practicals that require no philosophical training or reflection; we only need to learn from the experience of life. There are "laws of living that can be gleaned from ordinary everyday life." Stephen Covey, the popular author, maintains that personal effectiveness flows from the consistent application of principles that are universally found in the human experience. Covey describes principles as "deep, fundamental truths, classic truths, generic common denominators. They are tightly interwoven threads running with exactness, consistency, beauty and strength through the fabric of life."[16]

These principles for living, says Covey, have natural and unavoidable consequences: positive consequences when we are living in harmony with them, negative consequences when we spurn them. They apply to everyone, whether or not they live in awareness of them, but, Covey adds, "the more we know of correct principles, the greater our personal freedom to act wisely."[17]

Covey uses the example of "the law of the farm." In nature, the practice of cultivating the land is governed by natural processes and principles, and these principles determine outcomes. He asks, "Can you imagine forgetting to plant in the spring, flaking out all summer, and hitting it hard in the fall—ripping up the soil, throwing in the seeds, watering, cultivating—and expecting to get a bountiful harvest overnight?" Covey maintains that this kind of "cramming" not only fails in the natural world, it ultimately fails in a social system as well. Societies, Covey says, require careful conscientious cultivation. In the long run, the "law of the farm" governs in all arenas of life.[18]

The History of the Golden Rule

The Golden Rule is well suited as a standard for ordering society because it has roots in a wide range of world cultures and finds expression, in one form or another, in most if not all of the world's religions, as noted. The origins of the Golden Rule in Christianity are widely known. The first enunciation by Jesus of the Golden Rule is recorded in the Gospel of Matthew, where Jesus states: "So in everything, do to others what you would have them do to you, for this sums up the law and the prophets" (Matthew 7:12).

The Golden Rule found support throughout the whole of Christian history, including during the Middle Ages through the teachings of such church fathers as Augustine and Aquinas, during the Reformation in the writings of Luther and Calvin, and in modern America where it formed the core of Protestantism's social creed. Religious commentators have noted that a proper translation of the original Greek (*anthropoi*) in which the Golden Rule was first enunciated confirms that it was intended to govern relations between all people, not merely those of religious believers.

The Golden Rule is not, however, the exclusive product of Christianity, as already noted. Augustine, the great Christian theologian, extolled the Golden Rule as a universal principle that all cultures agreed on, not merely those grounded in revealed religion. Thus, the vision for finding unity via the Golden Rule at the level of social ethics while holding firmly to divergent theological convictions has enjoyed strong Christian backing throughout history, even among those whose doctrinal convictions have run the deepest.

This is true of devout religionists both inside and outside of Christianity. The earliest known religious formulations of the Golden Rule go back to Buddha and Confucius. For Confucius, the Golden Rule represented the ideal of character, self-discipline, and the selfless life. Also predating Christianity was the Jewish moral law and wisdom literature, which was replete with encouragement to pursue good and avoid evil through various maxims regarding family life, charity, and faithfulness to God.

In the ancient Hebrew scriptures, the Jewish believer is admonished to combine love of God with neighbor love. The command to "Love the Lord your God with all your heart, with all your soul and with all your strength" (Deuteronomy 6:5) was combined with "Love your neighbor as yourself" (Leviticus 19:18), much like the Christian formulation.

If the Golden Rule offers a basis for ethical unity and nearly universal integration amidst differing religious perspectives, it also operates independent of religion. The ancient Greeks, such as Plato, used reasoning much like that of the Golden Rule to develop general rules for the governance of society in such areas as the use of property and the conduct of commercial transactions. Early modern philosophers saw the Golden Rule as reflective of a "natural law," which existed independent of special revelation or divine grace, and accessible to all by virtue of its grounding in universal laws of nature.

With the rise of Rationalism, philosophers such as Thomas Hobbes treated the Golden Rule as a quite important, if not surprisingly useful social convention that individuals might consent to out of self-interest. Seen this way, individuals are free to apply (or violate) the Golden Rule as they wish in accordance with their own enlightened sense of interest. Those who live by the Golden Rule, Hobbes held, may expect to enjoy its rewards in the form of public praise and kind deeds reciprocated, while violators may be subjected to penalties ranging from social sanctions to personal guilt or loss of self-respect.

Although the Golden Rule has fallen out of widespread use as a basic rule for living, it is still seen by many within the field of ethics, in general terms at least, as a universal moral principle that enables individuals of all demographic backgrounds to engage in reasoned argument and to resolve conflict peacefully and effectively.

The Golden Rule in American History

The golden age of the Golden Rule on the American continent took place at the turn of the twentieth century as public officials, religious leaders, and businessmen alike popularized the Golden Rule as a means of coping with pressing social and moral conditions, including income disparities between rich and poor, urban squalor or rampant individualism.

Starting in the late 1900s, America found itself in the midst of numerous popular movements to promote the application of the Golden Rule, privately in the form of simple creeds, and publicly through literature, speeches, and popular slogans. The drive to elevate the Golden Rule as a universal social creed found especially strong support in the business and religious spheres.

The J.C. Penny Company, founded in 1875, stressed the importance of applying the Golden Rule to the everyday tasks of business. Mr. Penny was active in numerous lay movements throughout the Christian and civic community at the time, emphasizing the application of the Golden Rule.

Many businesses adopted the Golden Rule as their motto, seeking to accentuate the quality of a product or service, to display high ethical principle in the treatment of workers, or to merely advance civic improvement by means of promoting the brotherhood and service of mankind. Much of this public interest in the Golden Rule was inspired by a robust Protestantism that linked the simple logic of the Golden Rule to a social gospel of human betterment.[19]

In short, the Golden Rule has diverse religious as well as secular progeny and has functioned to promote human respect and dignity through human history. Though circumstances point to the possibility of a renewed embrace of the Golden Rule, and there are small signs of an awakening, no major movement has yet been launched to achieve its revitalization. The Golden Rule offers a simple, universal principle for a global community in search of unifying ideals.

Organizing a Golden Rule Movement

To revive interest in the Golden Rule in today's secular, pluralistic, and technological society, what models of action would be available to promote positive social change grounded in the Golden Rule? A Golden Rule movement would be organized around the popular model of society-wide "social movement," which seeks to achieve positive social change through voluntary, nonpolitical means and by methods designed to affect personal attitudes, beliefs, and behaviors. Such an initiative would be a broad-based, public education and awareness-raising initiative, enlisting opinion leaders across numerous fields and disciplines to participate in its work.

Values can and do shift in response to well-conceived, well-orchestrated efforts to affect attitudes and behaviors, centered especially on the recruitment of an ideologically diverse range of opinion leaders, as we have learned from numerous other social initiatives.

A public initiative centering on the Golden Rule would encourage the widest possible adoption of the Golden Rule, in both the public and the private sectors, as the most basic and universal life principle available for the ordering of human society. The social movement model, unlike models for political change, is ideologically diverse and it targets social and cultural centers of influence rather than the lawmaking process. The social movement contains elements (i.e., key opinion leaders) designed to affect elite fields and disciplines as well as grassroots movements. In short, this model of social change works within cultural and social mechanisms and is guided by up-to-date theories of how social values and attitudes take shape.

A Golden Rule initiative would recruit leaders from the key sectors of society—religion, politics, education, business, philanthropy, youth, civic, sports, and entertainment. These leaders will be coordinators and spokespersons within their sectors, developing sector-wide educational programs designed to raise awareness of the Golden Rule, as well as the practical tools for applying it. Those educational tools would include such things as public message campaigns, pledges, forums, resolutions, and public declarations.

A Golden Rule initiative would attempt to get businesses to adopt the Golden Rule as part of their marketing programs, incorporating the symbol and message of the Golden Rule in products and communications. Retailers could be urged to incorporate the Golden Rule message into point-of-purchase transactions. Restaurants could be encouraged to produce Golden Rule inserts in their window sales and table placements. Schools boards and school principals could be presented a short guide to turning their institutions into "Golden Rule Schools." Little League baseball clubs will be provided with a "Golden Rule Guide to Good Sportsmanship."

Each period in American history has witnessed the rise of well-conceived, carefully orchestrated public initiatives to promote a positive social good as the antidote to a particular social condition. The latter half of the twentieth century, for example, saw the rise of a civil rights movement which fundamentally altered how Americans think about race; a women's movement which dramatically shifted attitudes regarding the importance of women in all spheres of society; and an environmental movement which has shifted public sympathies in favor of conserving land, air, and water, and so on. Many other popular movements and campaigns have achieved deep and broad impact on such problems as smoking, drunk driving, or drug and alcohol abuse prevention, and family preservation.

Conclusion

That there is a deep and broad desire on the part of large majorities of the American people to restore at least minimal moral principles and laws for society has been well established. Drawing from America's rich and dynamic history of confronting moral and social problems through voluntary movements, a society-wide movement in the twenty-first century aimed at organizing civil society around the foundational principle of the Golden Rule could go far to humanize and harmonize what many have come to regard as a brutal and heartless society.

Notes

1. Daniel Yankelovich, "Trends in American Cultural Values," *Criterion* 35, no. 3 (Autumn 1996), 2-9.

2. Address by Vaclav Havel, Harvard University, Cambridge, June 8, 1995.

3. Havel, Harvard Address.

4. Robert Bellah et al., *The Good Society* (New York: Knopf, 1991), 114.

5. Amitai Etzioni, *The Spirit of Community* (New York: Touchstone, 1993), 2.

6. John Marks Templeton, *Worldwide Laws of Life* (Philadelphia: Templeton Foundation Press, 1993), 10.

7. Thomas Lickona, *Educating for Character* (New York: Bantam Books, 1992), 45.

8. Lickona, *Educating for Character*, 234.

9. Etzioni, *The Spirit of Community*, 12

10. Etzioni, 24.

11. James Q. Wilson, *The Moral Sense* (New York: Free Press, 1993), 2.

12. J. Budziszewski, "Natural Born Lawyers," *Weekly Standard*, December 20, 1999, 31.

13. C. S. Lewis, *The Abolition of Man* (New York: Macmillan, 1947), 84.

14. Lewis., *The Abolition of Man*, 77.

15. Budziszewski, "Natural Born Lawyers," 1.

16. Stephen Covey, *The Seven Habits of Effective People* (New York: Simon and Shuster, 1989), 122.

17. Covey, *Seven Habits*, 123.

18. Covey, 55.

19. For more read Jeffrey Wattles, *The Golden Rule* (New York: Oxford University Press, 1996).

Index

About the Authors

Don Eberly is a nationally recognized voice on issues of citizenship and civil society. His career includes over a decade of involvement in the nonprofit sector, where he founded several widely recognized civic organizations, including the National Fatherhood Initiative, and a decade of service in Washington, which included recently serving as Deputy Assistant to the President. He has written, coauthored, or edited seven books on issues of culture and society. He holds graduate degrees from George Washington University and Harvard University, and had affiliations with several national research institutes.

Ryan Streeter has written, edited, and contributed to several books on the public importance of the institutions of civil society. He authored the chapters in this book while serving as Research Fellow at Hudson Institute, where he actively contributed to the debate on the role of the voluntary sector for public life. Streeter currently serves in the White House Office of Faith-Based and Community Initiatives in Washington. He holds a Ph.D. from Emory University.